Life in Christ

by

NORMAN PITTENGER

WILLIAM B. EERDMANS PUBLISHING COMPANY
Grand Rapids, Michigan

241.36
P6P6e

183777

Preface

There comes a time for many of us when we want to set down as simply and clearly as possible a statement of what *really* matters for us, underneath and beyond everything else. This is so with me. I have spent my entire life as a teacher and student of Christian theology and have written many books about the subject; now, as I approach my seventieth year, I feel an urgent desire to communicate to the ordinary man or woman, not the professional scholar, what means most to me—not because I have any confidence that I am always right about everything (God forbid!) but because I am sure that such plain people who, like me, are trying to be disciples of Jesus Christ, can be helped when someone a little older tells them what has come to be central in his own life and experience.

For me that central reality is what I have called, using a phrase Paul employed scores of times, life "in Christ." This little book is my effort to say what that life really signifies, in terms of origins, characteristic features, the "enemies" to be fought by whoever seeks such life, the eternal expression of that life, and the goal which is before it. Throughout I have sought to be simple in style, clear in presentation, and concerned above all with communicating the truth of experience, as I have found it, to other men and women.

I happen to be an Episcopalian, but what I say is *not* "Episcopalian": it is, I sincerely believe, simply *Christian*—Evangelical Christianity, Catholic Christianity, Christianity as it can be lived by anybody, anywhere, anytime, who responds to the "love of God which was in Christ Jesus our Lord," from which "nothing can separate us."

—Norman Pittenger

Contents

1

The Foundation of Life in Christ

MANY PEOPLE WONDER WHAT IT MEANS TO BE A CHRIS-
tian—not just a nominal Christian but a *real* Christian, a
committed Christian, one who takes his allegiance to
Christ very very seriously.

Sometimes being a Christian is thought to mean "going
to church." That is important but it can hardly be called
the definition of Christian belonging. Sometimes it is
taken to mean acceptance of this or that creed or set of
doctrines. Firm belief is important but in itself is not the
definition of a Christian. Reading the Bible, saying one's
prayers, these two are sometimes assumed to make one a
Christian. Again, these are important but they do not
define a Christian. Let me propose an answer to the
question, What does it mean to be a Christian? which not
only makes sense of my own Christian allegiance but
which is founded upon the New Testament witness and
therefore ought to have a compelling quality for anyone
who dares to "profess and call himself Christian."

To be a Christian is *to be caught up into life in Christ.*
Life in Christ gives their importance to church-going,
doctrines, creeds, Bible reading, prayer—and maybe above
all to the effort day by day to live with one's fellowmen
in a fashion befitting the man or woman who would be a
disciple of Jesus.

In Paul's letters, New Testament experts tell us, the

Apostle uses the phrase "in Christ" about a hundred times. He uses the phrase in many different connections, and a superficial reading might lead one to think that sometimes it is just tagged on to a sentence without any specific purpose. But such a reading is mistaken. Wherever and whenever Paul uses the words "in Christ" he is talking about some aspect of the Christian life of redeemed discipleship which is absolutely central to his thinking because first of all it has been central in his experience as a converted man. When he speaks of being "found in Christ" and elsewhere says that "For me to live *is* Christ," to take two examples, he is telling us this: here and now the Christian is living in a certain specific relationship; and this relationship is increasingly to be realized, so that finally he will discover that the little preposition *in* has become the very truth of his existence. The Christian will find himself "*in* Christ" because he has been found *by* Christ and been given the life which nothing, not even death, can destroy. For the Apostle himself, it was his experience of conversion on the Damascus Road which began this process; the rest of his life had been a working out of the process in his day-by-day relationships, whatever these may have been. Everything had been made radically different for him through the new principle of life which was given him with his conversion—and that new principle was nothing other than life in Christ, his Saviour, his Lord, and his Master.

The exact phrase "in Christ" does not appear in John's Gospel nor in the letters of John. But the insistence on what I have sometimes ventured to call "the en-Christed life" is plainly there. For example, in Jesus' "table talk" in John 13-16 the disciples are told that they are "the branches" and Jesus "the vine." The image is different from the one used by Paul; the intention is surely the same. Those who are Christ's are to have his life in them, as the life of the vine is in its branches; only so can they truly live and "bring forth much fruit." Again, in the

"High Priestly Prayer" which is the seventeenth chapter of John's Gospel, Jesus prays that his disciples will be "in him" and he "in them," as the Father is "in him" and he is "in the Father." Here is the most intimate of relationships, which is identical in significance with the Pauline "life in Christ." And in John's First Letter the wonderful fourth chapter is all about Christian discipleship as so much "in Christ," who is God's Love come to men, that to live "in love" *is* to live "in Christ" precisely because "God loved us and sent his Son into the world, that we might live through him."

For centuries Christians have spoken about living "in grace" or "in the Spirit"—and here both Paul and John have been the source for such thinking. But the familiar words in II Corinthians 13:14 bring all this together: "the grace of our Lord Jesus Christ and the love of God and the fellowship of the Holy Spirit." "Life in Christ" and "life in grace" are the same thing; "life in the Spirit" and "life in Christ" are also the same thing. What we really have here are three ways of speaking about a single reality, known so profoundly in Christian experience, and spelled out in various ways. To be a Christian *is* to be alive in Christ, by his strength and favor ("grace"), through the empowering activity of the Spirit whom Christ sends and gives. The inner life of the Christian is marked by a new quality; he is thus different from other men, whether they are good men or evil men. His external conduct is motivated and animated by that inner principle; other people see that these Christians are indeed "different." But the word "principle" is too impersonal; it is Jesus Christ himself who "dwells in them and they in him," so that men "take notice of them that they have been with Jesus."

The subject of this book is this "life in Christ." We shall consider the "place" where it can be known, the Spirit who empowers it, the nourishment given to it, its several characteristic features, the antagonists against which it must contend, the way in which it is summed up in Paul's triad of "faith, hope, and love," and the ultimate goal or end towards which it moves. But first of all we must think about a few preliminary matters, more particularly the "grounding" of life in Christ, its necessary foundation or base. Unless we look at this we cannot understand what this life is all about.

The life in Christ is grounded in the event in human history which we call by the name of Jesus. In a moment I shall explain why I have phrased the matter in that fashion. But for now, let us see that the possibility of life in Christ is established through something God has done at a given time and in a given place. Let us also see that the sort of life which is "in Christ" is the sort of life which Christ himself lived in "the days of his flesh."

The New Testament communicates to us all that we really know about this. The stories it tells about Jesus in the Gospels are not meant to be biographical, as if reporters had been on hand to take notes on what was said and done for the benefit of future writers. The stories are all told "from faith to faith," to use a Pauline phrase. They refer to incidents and sayings in Jesus' career, not for their possible biographical interest but because through these incidents and sayings a response in faith may be evoked in those who hear them. The stories were first repeated within the Christian community as part of its preaching and teaching; then, years later, they were written down. Whatever difficulty some scholars find in the details of incident and saying, the *big* thing is clear: Jesus was like this, he spoke like this, he acted like this, he lived like this. It is the overall picture, the total impact, which matters most; it is the response in commitment through faith in that Figure which is desired and expected, above and beyond anything else. To this we shall come back time and again.

Now we live in a world which is continually in a process of change. Things happen in that world and those things make a difference, have consequences in what happens afterward. There was a time when most people thought that the world was static, with only insignificant rearrangements of bits of matter in new patterns. In a world like that things would "stay put," although the way which that "staying-put" looked like might not always be the same. But that mechanistic kind of naturalism, popular in the nineteenth century, is completely dead nowadays; the various sciences no longer talk in that fashion. A mechanical interpretation of evolutionary process, seen as only a further application of old Newtonian physics, has very few, if any, defenders among the best scientific investigators and philosophers.

But in the minds of many ordinary people, something like that outdated idea hangs on. What is more, there remain among us the remnants of an even earlier view—which goes back for hundreds, even thousands, of years. That view assumed that the world had been created a long time ago and been put on a path which it followed without deviation except for occasional intrusions of God into it by miracles which (on such a view) had to be taken as "violations" of established "natural law." Intrusions like that were not typical of "how things really go in the normal course of events"; they were acts of the *deus ex machina,* "a God out of a machine."

Instead of seeing things this way, great modern thinkers insist that the world is continually *being created,* with new happenings that have a fresh and unexpected quality about them. Ours is a *living* universe and history is a *living* movement; in each area there are novelties, new factors, new possibilities, and these *make a difference.*

The reader may wonder how the last few paragraphs fit into the subject of this book. The answer is clear enough. A world like that, where new things happen which make a difference, yet in which there is continuity of purpose and direction, is a world in which what I have called "the event in human history," which the name Jesus indicates,

has a place. In one sense that event is the culmination of
everything that happened before it, both in Jewish history and in the wider history of the human race (here we
must remember that Judaism was never isolated from the
rest of men's history and experience and that what took
place outside the limits of Judaism proper was enormously influential in what took place within it). But the
event of Christ not only brought to flower what had gone
before. It was also a genuinely *new* event in the world's
story. It had an *over-plus* of meaning which could not be
explained simply by reference to Jewish beliefs nor by
noting that elsewhere there had been preparation for and
parallels with the event. Indeed "parallels" is the wrong
word here; what we have are hints and intimations which
are given fulfilment in what Jesus said and did and what
his disciples believed he had accomplished in history and
the world. If the new event were to be explained, it
required for that explanation recognition that in it God
had been especially at work. That special work of God
made life in Christ a possibility; the life *of* Christ, where
God had so actively revealed himself, had established for
men the life *in* Christ, where they would find reconciliation and fulfilment.

Not that God had been absent from his creation before
that event. God was *always* active in his creation, providing for it the goals which it was to seek, the continuing
lure to decide for those goals, and the final satisfaction or
enjoyment of those goals once they were reached—a
satisfaction or enjoyment in which God himself would
share. And there had been wrong decisions, mistaken
choices, backwaters or deviations in the ongoing of the
creation, as "the creatures" went astray from the divine
purpose. In men there had been even worse: there had
been wilfulness and pride which not only damaged those
who were guilty of them but disastrously affected others
and the future—there had been *sin* with its appalling
consequences. Yet God never deserted his creation; he

always worked to bring good out of evil, love out of hate, righteousness out of injustice, beauty out of ugliness and disharmony.

Hence it would be mistaken to think of the event of Christ as *absolutely* new, as if God had "changed his mind" and done something utterly out of character; but it is right to think of it as *genuinely* new, its novelty the intensifying or focusing in a single set of happenings, at a particular time and place, of what God is always and everywhere "up to" in his creation. It was like the concentration of the rays of the sun in a reading glass, bringing about novel results—for example, setting fire to a piece of cloth or paper. The novel result with which we are concerned in this book is life in Christ.

I said earlier that I would explain why I used the phrase "the event of Christ." The explanation is twofold. First, the phrase is being used to stress the fact that in this world of ours, and in our human experience within it, we have to do with occurrences or happenings much more than with *things* that can simply be located in this or that spot and might seem entirely self-contained. In truth, as even modern physics has taught us if our own experience had not already made it clear, the world and life are a continuing series of occurrences in which energy is concentrated and given particular point. And man is not a *thing;* he is an ongoing movement, bringing together physical, mental, and emotional drives so that they move forward towards goals.

That brings me to my second reason for using the phrase "the event of Christ." Any and every event or happening in the world has three aspects, as a little reflection will make plain. First, it gathers up what has gone before, all the influences of the past which have made its appearance possible. Second, it is related with everything that is going on around it, in ordinary contacts, in contemporary history, and in the most far-ranging cosmic or natural environment. Third, it has consequences or results, bringing about changes which otherwise would have been impossible. I am reminded of Robert Frost's poem about the choice of a road when he found himself one day at a crossroads; he chose one road, not the other, and (as he says) "*that* has made the difference."

Thus an event is a meeting of the past, the present, and the future, at one point of time. If we try to take the past only, we lose sight of the novelty of the event; if we try to take the present alone, we become victims of sheer contemporaneity; and if we try to take the future alone, we become silly utopians. Anybody can see how the importance of conserving the past can then be corrupted into unyielding reactionary attitudes, the importance of recognizing the present corrupted into mere faddishness, and the importance of looking to the future corrupted into an unrealistic flight of fancy. When past, present, and future are taken together, we have a healthy balance.

What is true generally of events is also true in respect to Jesus Christ. We can so think of him that Christian discipleship becomes an attempt to imitate his exact ways of acting—forgetful of the Spirit who, he said, would "lead us into all truth" and (in Lowell's words) on "new occasions" "teach new duties." Or we can so think of him as our "contemporary" (which of course he is, but not in *this* way) that we forget the revealed nature of his will and goal when he dwelt in Palestine—and then we are likely to be swayed by our own ideas of what is right and good. Or we can so think of him as "ahead of us," understood only as what some moderns call "our future," that he is irrelevant to our concrete present situation with all its difficulties and all its promise.

But when we say "the event of Christ" we naturally and rightly center our attention on the Man who lived in Palestine and rose from the dead "on the third day." To know about him we must turn to the New Testament. Yet the New Testament cannot be understood without

reference to the Old Testament and its reflection of
God's way with the people of Israel in the "older dispensation." Nor can it be understood without reference to
the actual situation in Palestine in Jesus' own day and to
the response made to Jesus by those who met him, heard
him, followed him, or rejected him. Finally it cannot be
understood apart from what it has affected, as a matter
of fact, in the ages which have followed. Jesus, as the
New Testament portrays him, is the center in which that
past is summed up, those contemporary relationships
experienced, and that resultant future given significance
and explanation.

What it comes down to is this. Had that event not
taken place, there could be no possibility, for men now
or at any time, to enjoy the wonderful richness of life in
Christ which, as we shall see again and again, is life in *love,*
or better in *Love* (the upper-case "L" indicating that it is
in *God* who, as John tells us, *is* Love). Of course there
could have been good moral lives, even lives which had a
loving nature—but not that kind or quality of sheer
outgoing love which was in Christ the Man and is im-
parted to those who are enabled to live *in* him. This is
what Christianity is basically all about. Through Jesus
Christ men have been reconciled to God and with their
fellows. Continuing to accept and respond to such reconciliation, they live in a different way. It may not always
be obvious; certainly the principle is hidden in the inner
heart, but it is *there,* inescapably and gloriously. And for
its origin we look to him who lived among us "full of
grace and truth"—of grace, divine favor and empowering;
of truth, in terms of the way the world *really* goes in and
under God. It is through the achievement which God
wrought in Christ, a work which in Christopher Smart's
splendid words from his poem *The Son of David* was
"determined, dared, and done" there and then in that
Man, that Christian existence is given to God's children.
The historical center is there, but it is not a matter of the

"dead past." Indeed there is no "dead past," since (as we have urged) *every* event has its continuing living consequences and once it has taken place nothing remains unaltered. Above all in *this* event, what was wrought in the past is an experienced fact in the present as Christ's followers live in him who is their Saviour.

We come to know the event in its historical center as we read the Scriptures, hear the Word in the proclamation of the gospel, have communion with Christ in the Lord's Supper, and in meditation and prayer let our minds dwell on him. The One who is remembered is, through the Spirit, a living Presence in the here and now of our experience in the twentieth century.

There is the other side, too. As this One is remembered, known, and adored, the life which is in him reflects, in our own time and under our own conditions, the same quality of life which marked his days so long ago. In the contemporary Christian man or woman that quality is reproduced, however feebly and imperfectly. How can we come to understand what this means? I suggest that our best analogy is drawn from the human experience of love between two persons. Augustine saw this to be so; and he once said that only a "lover" could comprehend its significance. When I love another truly and deeply, and as unselfishly as my sinful manhood will permit, my life finds in him its center and point of reference. I am committed to him, I give myself to him as he has done to me, I look for great things from him, I am united to him in the very depths of my being—and I find myself wonderfully fulfilled and enriched. Some dim awareness of this glorious fact speaks through popular songs; a glimpse of it brings joy and at the same time a feeling of unworthiness (who am I, that I should be privileged to be loved and to love in return?). The intensity of our love may vary enormously; but the reality of it is undeniable. None of us has arrived at its fulness; all of us trust that we are moving towards that fulness.

And when two persons are thus bound in love, each begins to reflect something of the other's quality of life. The mutual indwelling leads us not to "ape" the other but to be *ourselves* in relationship with him. There is a sort of contagion of spirit, through which each "catches" from the other this or that facet of the love which unites us. Then my thinking and acting and feeling are like his; his are like mine.

"If ye then, being stingy, know how to give good gifts, . . . how much more God?" We are weak, imperfect, and sinful; hence a relationship such as I have just described is weak, imperfect, and too often marked by the wrongness which we call "sin." But the analogy holds; and we have Jesus' own permission to employ human analogies for the things of God—the loving Father, the good Shepherd, the sovereign Ruler, glimpsed through human fatherhood, shepherding, and ruling, with all their imperfection. So it is that in relationship with Christ, and with God in and through Christ, there is commitment of self to the Lord, a friendship so profound that love is the only word adequate to describe it. There is expectation of "great things" which God will do in Christ; equally there is God's expectation of "great things" which we may do for him, in Christ. There is a sharing or mutuality, for the Lord of our lives is always giving to us and he also wants from us the one gift we can bring—"ourselves, our souls and bodies," as a "reasonable, holy, and lively sacrifice." He wants also our sins, repented of and mourned for, so that he can use even human wrongdoing for a greater good. And there is the path to fulfilment as the Christian offers himself to do what Paul dared to call "making up that which is lacking in the sufferings [really this should be translated, "the experience"] of Christ for his Body's sake, which is the church." Not that his Lord is weak and asks for help, but that the man who is "in Christ" knows that he can offer that Lord opportunity for wider expression of his purpose, fuller manifestation of his love, by free human consent given in faith: "be it unto me according to thy word."

Because this happens, the true "imitation of Christ" is made possible. This is no copying of the exact details of the Master's life in Palestine as these have been recorded in the Gospels. If that were the case, "imitation" would be irrelevant to us who do not live in agricultural first-century Palestine but in the confusing, noisy, industrial twentieth century with all it offers us of "weal and woe." To "imitate Christ" in this century of ours is to be grasped by his Spirit, filled with his energy, open to the contagion of his life, which then can be manifested in the very different times in which we live and in ways that may very well be different from his specific ways in the "days of his flesh." Yet the abiding reference is always to the historic life and to the total event of which that life was the very heart and center, with its characteristic pattern of thought, feeling, and action.

I have just used the word "pattern"; and I did it deliberately. For I was thinking of the way in which the great Danish Christian of the last century, Søren Kierkegaard, constantly spoke of Jesus as our "pattern," to be reproduced in our lives, or even better re-presented (not merely *represented,* but presented once again and in a fresh fashion), day by day in our own thought, feeling, and action. But not only the "pattern"—Jesus is also *the power* making the re-presentation possible for those who live in him.

One last point must be made before this opening chapter ends. Life *in* Christ has both a Godward and a manward direction, just as the life *of* Christ had that same double direction. It is life *with God* in Christ, a direction made possible by what God has done in him, giving himself in love for us and thus showing that "his nature and his name is Love," as Wesley puts it so beautifully in one of his hymns. It is life *with men* in Christ, a direction opened to those who are caught up into that self-giving love which was "en-manned," "en-fleshed," incarnate in our Lord and Saviour, who gave himself as "a ransom for many," not just for a select few. In Christ, as the great contemporary theologian Karl Barth used to insist, God "elected" all men as his own, by the very fact that in his Son he "elected *that* Man."

Thus life in Christ is not an individualistic matter. No human life could really be that anyway, for we belong together as men in a *social* world which is the other side of, and equally important as, our *personal* existence. The Christian knows this even more profoundly: he is not only bound up in "one bundle of life," as the Old Testament has it, with all other men; he also has a more intimate and immediate sharing with others who, like him, live in Christ. The next chapter will consider this social aspect of life in Christ, particularly in relationship to the Christian fellowship or community of faith which we know as the Church of the living Christ.

2

The Situation of Life in Christ

IN THE PREVIOUS CHAPTER WE NOTED THAT PAUL USES the phrase "in Christ" some one hundred times and that for him the Christian life can be described as "living in Christ": "For me to live *is* Christ." Now we must point out that the Apostle also speaks time and again of the Christian community or fellowship as "the Body of Christ." Every Christian is a "member" of the Body whose Head is Christ himself.

Thus in the twelfth chapter of First Corinthians he speaks of the faithful as "baptized into one body," while in the twelfth chapter of Romans he says that his Christian correspondents in the capital city of the Roman Empire are, with him and all other Christians, "one body in Christ, and individually members one of another." Writing to the Colossian Christians he reminds them that Christ is "the head of the body, the Church," in which he himself is a minister "according to the divine office" given him, so that all may be "nourished and knit together" in the Head of the Body. Again, he warns the Corinthians in his first letter to them that if they come to the Lord's Supper "unworthily" they "eat and drink judgment" unto themselves because they "do not discern the body"—which here certainly means, not the eucharistic elements but the Christian fellowship which unworthy Christians have offended by their selfishness and lack of concern. Finally, to conclude this brief selection from his writings, Paul (New Testament scholars are divided on the question of whether Paul wrote this particular epistle) tells the Ephesian Christians that they are to see their calling as a "growing up in every way into him who is the head, even Christ, from whom the whole body, joined and knit together by every joint with which it is supplied . . . grows as a body and upbuilds itself in love."

Christ is the Head, Christians his members—it is like John's vine-branch analogy. Christ and his members make up the total Body of Christ. His members live in him as their Head. What it comes down to is simply this: for Paul a Christian is one who as a "member of Christ" lives in him, as Christ lives in his faithful people. The man who would be a disciple must therefore of necessity be part of the Body "which is the Church."

For the Apostle to the Gentiles, for the Beloved Disciple, and for the whole New Testament witness, although they expressed it in differing ways, there was no possibility of full Christian discipleship except through membership in the Church. The situation in which the life in Christ was given and realized was the Christian community or fellowship. Conversely, membership in that fellowship *was* life in Christ, however partial or imperfect may have been the awareness men had of that enormous privilege and however inadequately they fulfilled the responsibilities it brought with it.

The New Testament writers, Paul above all, were keenly conscious of the failure, sin, and error of members of the community. They were under no illusions about wavering loyalty; they saw clearly the mistakes and wrong decisions made by them and their fellow-sharers in the life in Christ. And although they did not use these words, they were under no illusion about the fact that as a sociological phenomenon, a visible society of men and women, the Church was very far from perfect. Even in those days of the "first fine, careless rapture" of Chris-

tian discipleship; even with the much less complicated
ecclesiastical apparatus, in comparison with what we see
and know; even with an enthusiasm which we can only
wish we were able to emulate—the observable association
of Christians, both individually and as a group, left very
much to be desired. And one of the points most often
stressed in the Epistles is precisely this defection from the
high calling of Christian profession.

Nonetheless, despite all that was wrong with the community of the faithful as they saw it and shared in it, the
New Testament writers consistently witness to the necessity of common sharing in the fellowship. They knew
that it was that fellowship which was Christ's Body, that
it was that fellowship which proclaimed the gospel of his
saving power and reconciling love, that it was that fellowship which "broke the bread" at the Lord's Supper or
Eucharist, and that it was that fellowship which cared for
the afflicted, the troubled, the poor, the needy. That was
one reason for their loyalty to the Church. There was also
another. Their Jewish background made them keenly
aware of the fact that no man does or can live "from
himself" and "by himself." For a Jew the very fact of his
Jewishness meant that he was a member of "the chosen
people" and that only so did he live by, and in, *Torah*—
God's revealed will for that people. A Jew apart from
Judaism was unthinkable; this is still true for modern
Jews. From its parent Christianity inherited this sense of
corporate belonging; but now it was no longer a matter of
belonging to the "older dispensation" chosen by God,
but to the "new dispensation in the Spirit" effected by
God's act in Christ and fulfilling the hopes, aspirations,
and dreams of the older Israel. The Christian community
was God's gift, his work, not man's accomplishment and
certainly not a casual association of men and women who
easily could have been Christian believers in isolation
from the brethren.

The modern notion of "individuality" was unknown at

the time, not only among the Jews but elsewhere in the ancient world. We may even say that this notion is a product of the Christian centuries, or at least a product of Christian civilization. Sometimes it has been perverted; and the very word, as I have suggested earlier, suggests false ideas. But the truth for which it can stand is the growing awareness of your and my distinctive *personality,* with our duties, responsibilities, opportunities, defects, wrongdoings. It goes wrong when it is thought to mean separation from the brethren, or "self-conscious isolation" from others. This last mistake is derived from certain philosophical ideas about what was styled "individual substance" during the centuries right after the Renaissance and Reformation. And that is most certainly a distortion of the truth, which like all such distortions is the more dangerous because it is a twisting of genuine truth and has a certain seductive attraction. But this is all incidental; my point is simply that in the ancient world men were keenly aware of belonging together in what modern scholars have sometimes aptly described as "corporate personality."

Nowadays thoughtful people know that everything in the creation is in relationship with everything else. Everything affects, and is affected by, everything else. And this general truth has its very special illustration in our human situation. Each of us is dependent upon, because he belongs to, the total environment about him; and especially he is dependent upon, because he is part of, the totality of humanity. I am thus dependent on friends and neighbors, the people among whom I live, the family in which I was born and brought up, those whom I love and who love me, the country of which I am a citizen, the civilization to which I belong, the labors of people whom I have never seen. By an extension of this fact, I am dependent upon the earth itself, from which comes the food I eat, the drink I require, the clothing I wear, the materials from which my home is built, the weather I must enjoy or endure . . . and so much else that the list could be endless. But my particular dependence is upon other people; it is through and with them that I have learned to think, to speak, to express myself. And I have begun to realize my personal selfhood precisely through this whole series of relationships.

But the collective or community character of existence does not resemble an ant-hill, in which I am "lost in the crowd." Nor is it a mere aggregation of many men. Hence neither "rugged individualism," with its doctrine of "each man for himself," nor totalitarianism, with its doctrine that this or that man has no secure rights to his own manhood, is possible in the long run; and in a way recent history has demonstrated this, with the collapse of nations which were too intent on the individual's claims as well as those which were too intent on totalitarian pressures.

All this is highly relevant to Christian profession. The Christian community is a fulfilment of man's natural tendency to live together with his brethren. It is also a divine achievement which is meant to crown that human community-life and correct its defects due to selfishness and man's pride and wrongness. The Christian community has its supreme loyalty to Christ himself, seen always as the decisive action of God to reveal himself to men and to open for them a deep relationship with himself. Its character as a community is the reflection in the life of our world of the distinctive kind of love which is disclosed by and released through Christ. Its purpose is to bring more and more men into this relationship so that the love there released may be more widely shared and more truly effective in every aspect of human affairs. This is the sort of vision which in their own way and with their own words the earliest Christians accepted and gloried in.

This, then, is the situation in which the life in Christ is known and shared. And this is why we shall now try to sketch the nature of that fellowship in its true reality. What is its "form" or its "structure"? What are the particular features which have given it identity through the centuries from its earliest days down to the present hour? These are important questions; we need to have some answer to them, because they will help us understand better the situation in which life in Christ is given to men.

But before we speak of these "forms" or "structures," we need first of all to grasp the truth that the Church is no *static* society, with all of its details completely fixed. In that case it would not be a community or a fellowship, but would resemble a machine with its several parts, each of them playing some necessary role in making the machine do its proper work. The Church is like every other living reality in our world, with its continuity with the past, its relationships in the present, and its forward thrust towards the realizing of its goal or aim. The Church, we might well say, is a living social process in history—I have written a book about this, entitled in fact *The Church as Social Process*. In that book I tried to show how the Church lives *from* its past, remembering unfailingly the event from which it took its origin, Jesus Christ and all that his name signifies; and how it lives *in* the present, working today to bring to the world the saving power of Jesus Christ and conform that world to the love which in him was shed abroad in human life; and how it lives *towards* the future, as it "prepares and makes ready the way" for God's Kingdom, which he will bring in his good time. As such a process or movement, the Christian fellowship moves down through the ages; and those who share in it, and hence live in Christ, are caught up into that movement and enabled to act as its personal agencies as it carries on its work.

But like all living movements, it has a pattern which enables us to see more clearly what it is and why it is. I believe we can say that this pattern is fourfold: (1) faith

in Christ professed and practiced; (2) proclamation of his
gospel; (3) sacramental "means of grace" through which
Christian people are nourished in Christ's life and offer
themselves to his service; and (4) the outward and visible
ways in which it re-presents and makes effective in the
world the love of God which it both knows and cele-
brates.

Many Christians would wish to add a fifth: a ministry
continuous from the first days of the fellowship. I should
agree about the importance of such a ministry, however
we picture it. Some would talk about a succession
through the episcopate; others would stress a succession
through eldership or the presbyterate; and still others
would lay their emphasis on the discipleship of the whole
Church expressed through men or women "called" to
function for it. What is essential is that there is *some* sort
of continuity with the very first days in the maintenance
of the "Apostles' fellowship and of prayer"; the particular form is less central. But I shall not discuss this question, since it is much more a matter of theological than of
practical concern. Such ministerial continuity, however,
like the other four which I have noted, has its value or
worth in the degree to which it effectively serves the
purpose of maintaining some identifiable pattern for the
community as that community does its great work of
bringing life in Christ to the children of men who are the
beloved children of God their Father. If any of these
modes or agencies fails to do this, it needs radical modifi-
cation in some way or other. The great reforming movements in Christian history have had as their main objective a correction of defects in these agencies, a return to
their primitive significance and use, and a fresh vision of
the fellowship as indeed Christ's Body which is here to do
Christ's work of enlivening, quickening, inspiring, pardon-
ing, enabling, and reconciling.

Let us then look briefly at the four I have mentioned:
the community's faith, its proclamation of the gospel, its

celebration of the sacraments (and here we shall be concerned especially with Baptism and the Lord's Supper, the Holy Communion, the Eucharist—call it what you will), and its manifestation of the love of God in Christ to the world about it.

First there is the Church's faith. We are talking here about the community's commitment to the decisive moment in the past, when in the event of Jesus Christ God acted in human history with an intensity elsewhere unknown, in order to disclose his nature as love, his activity in the world in love, his concern for his human children whom he unfailingly and faithfully loves, and his acceptance of them in love—reconciling them to himself in Christ. The Church in this respect is the place where this response in faith takes place. Or, as Martin Luther once said, it is the place "where justification by grace through faith is known." Because of its faith, it can be open to God's Spirit and become also the place, the situation, in which life in Christ may be lived.

Second, the proclamation of the gospel. Because the Church lives by its faith, it must proclaim or bear witness to the good news of God's act in Christ, in response to which this faith has been awakened. The proclamation may be made in many ways, by deed as well as by word. Often we think of the sermon, or of evangelistic preaching, as the principal way in which the proclamation is made. Certainly preaching is *one* of the ways—and its importance cannot be minimized, for as the preacher "breaks the Bread of Life," interpreting the scriptural witness to his Lord, he is enabled by the Spirit's power to bring his hearers into the very presence of his Lord so that they may be caught up in the response of living faith. But unordained men and women may proclaim the gospel by the chance word, the occasional testimony, and above all by their way of living out what they believe. It may be that this witness, by deeds of love, sympathy, understanding, helpfulness, openness to others, is the most effective method of making the proclamation. But whatever the means chosen, the proclamation is the same: "God was in Christ reconciling the world unto himself." There, in the Man of Nazareth, God acted decisively—but always in a fashion characteristic of himself as "pure unbounded love"—on men's behalf to bring them to himself and enable them to have fellowship with him in "the Man of God's own choosing."

Third, the celebration of the sacraments. The "gospel sacraments," as the great Reformers liked to put it, are two: Baptism and the Lord's Supper. Around these many ancient Christian groups have included others, such as "confirmation," the declaration of God's forgiveness of sin, etc. Baptism is entrance into the Christian community; it is the way a man becomes "a member of Christ." Once received, it leaves its mark upon the man, and no Christian should forget that he has been baptized. Luther said a wonderful thing about this. He remarked that when he was depressed about himself and his failures, he always reminded himself that he had been baptized; it made all the difference to recall this tremendous fact. The Lord's Supper is the way in which the fellowship obeys its Lord's command, is united with him in abiding communion, offers itself to him again and again for him to use as he will, and is strengthened to go forth in his service in the world. The Word, or the message of the gospel which is proclaimed in spoken word or in deed, is in the Lord's Supper planted in our hearts as we receive, in faith and with thanksgiving, the bread and wine which Christ took and blessed, broke and gave, to his disciples in the Upper Room on the night before he was betrayed—and commanded, as they believed, that they should do this again and again "in remembrance of him."

Fourth, manifestation in action in the world. Here we have to do with Christian conduct or behavior, with attitudes as well as actions. The community bears its witness by what it does, through its members, in the affairs of daily life, in the big matters and the small, to declare God's loving concern, his healing power, and his forgiveness and acceptance of his erring children. This is the external or visible expression, which men can see and hear, of the life in Christ in which the fellowship's members share. It is social and personal—social because it is personal, and personal because it has a social outreach.

Now all that is done in and by the Christian fellowship is by "the power of the Holy Spirit." We shall see in our next chapter how the Spirit enables us to respond in faith, inspires the proclamation of the gospel, makes the celebration of the sacraments effective, and impels the community and its members to external Christian witness. Here we need only remark that recognition of the Spirit's work in each of these aspects of the Church's existence delivers the community from any pretension to its own merit. The stress on the Spirit is a safeguard against Pelagianism, that old heresy which seemed to say that human effort in and of itself would induce God to act; whereas the truth is that God comes first, always first, to awaken, stimulate, strengthen, and solicit what man, and the community of men, may do in his service. The Church is thus preserved from the horrible pride which so often attacks institutions; it knows that it is indeed the Body of Christ, but it also knows its weakness, fallibility, and liability to distort the truth which God has entrusted to it. Everything it does is done by men, of course; but by men towards God, in Christ, and by the power of the Spirit.

It is possible for someone to accept many if not all of the beliefs that are held by the Christian Church, to observe many of the moral principles which the Christian fellowship teaches, and to act frequently in a way which may put church members to shame—and still not to *belong*. Yet it is by the diffused influence of the Christian Church through the centuries that these beliefs are accept-

ed, these principles observed, and this standard of conduct followed. On the other hand, very few thoughtful
and devout Christians who do belong would deny that
the community itself is always in need of reformation.
Even Roman Catholics today are using the old Latin
phrase, *ecclesia semper reformanda,* "the Church must
always be reforming." Sometimes it is the statement of
faith, couched in language that makes little if any sense
to modern people, which is in need of restatement so that
its basic assertions may become crystal clear. Sometimes
its way of stating its moral principles reminds one of the
legalism from which Christ came to deliver God's children
into a new freedom under God's "unwritten law in their
hearts." Sometimes it is the ways in which the Church's
worship is conducted that make it seem antiquated and
out of touch with reality as people experience it in our
own time. Always it is the problem of effectively bringing
its members to act as befits their Christian profession, in
business and social affairs, in race relations, in the realms
of politics and international relations. Here there is need
for reformation, rethinking, reconception. Of course this
is the case; most of us know it very well.

But this does not mean that I can contemplate rejection of membership in the community or that I can sever
myself from it if I am already a member. If I really wish
to live in Christ, the place where this becomes possible
for me is precisely that community, with all its faults and
imperfections. Even when it has been at its worst, the
Church has not forgotten its faith, failed somehow to
proclaim the gospel, stopped the celebration of its sacraments, and entirely ceased to make some witness, however feeble, to Christ in the world. It may be that my
own participation in its life, if I am truly in earnest about
it, can do a little to help the Church, humanly speaking,
make the changes which are needed; while, at the same
time, I must be humble enough to see that such participation may do a great deal for me. R. H. Tawney, the

English Christian economist of the earlier years of this century, once warned that "the man who seeks God in separation from his brethren is likely to find, not God, but the devil, whose countenance will bear a surprising resemblance to his own face." We need to take that warning to heart.

So I bring this chapter to a close by repeating my insistence that the man or woman who wishes to share the life in Christ will find that the place where, the situation in which, that sharing is normally available is the Christian community. By taking part in its life, by humbly yet not uncritically giving it his support, he will indeed "grow in grace" and deepen his "knowledge and love of God" in Christ Jesus. *Love:* that is the key word. Let us remember always that love *means* "relationship"; no man can love without others whom he in fact *does* love. In intention and much more in fact than some readily admit, the Christian community is the fellowship of love, where relationships are established in which love may be expressed and deepened.

In one of Edmund Spenser's poems we are told that "Love is the lesson that the Lord us taught." The Lord taught us this lesson in word, but above all in deed. And the love had to do with God himself, who *is* Love; it had to do with the action of God in the total event we name when we say Christ; it had to do with the frightening truth that every son of man has received from God the vocation to become a lover, by God's grace and in Christ's power; it had to do with the encouraging truth that through the Holy Spirit we may become those lovers we are being created to become. And by no means least, it had to do with the establishment in the world of human history of a community whose purpose is to live in love, to show love, and to help men to learn to love.

Thus if the life in Christ is truly life in Love—and once again I use the upper-case "L," since I am speaking of life with *God* in Christ—then it is required of us that we "love the brethren." In John's First Letter, the stress on love in the wonderful fourth chapter has its first reference, as a careful reading will show, to the Christian community itself, to membership in it, and life within it. We are then to love "our even Christians," as Mother Julian of Norwich put it: those who with us are "churchmen," members of the Body of Christ. We are to accept them, live with them, learn from them, in the community of lovers-in-the-making where God's love in Christ is believed, celebrated and, to however small or great degree, manifested in act. In that fellowship life in Christ is offered; and then, by its overflowing into every nook and cranny of human existence together in the world, life in Christ will be reflected in all we say and think and do. Such is the logic of love, as Christians learn it in the Church, the place where life in Christ is experienced and made effective for men.

3

The Empowering Spirit of Life
in Christ

IN THE LAST CHAPTER THE NECESSITY OF THE CHRIS-
tian community was stressed; we insisted, on the basis of
the New Testament witness, that this community is the
place where, the situation in which, life in Christ is to be
known and experienced. Of course Christ is not *limited*
to the fellowship, as if it confined his presence and work
to one and only one channel or process in human history.
Christ is, Christ works, where and as he wills; sometimes
he does this in the most unlikely and unexpected places.
But normally and as the consequence of what Old and
New Testaments would call God's "covenant" with or
abiding promise to his children, it is in the fellowship that
we are given assurance of the life "which is life indeed."

Particularly in our day, when so many reject the
Church altogether, not simply because of its failures and
imperfections but because of the Church's sheer "irrele-
vance" to our modern conditions, such a "high" view of
the Christian community may strike the reader as odd.
No longer is the Church the arbiter of morals, the magis-
trate of accepted teaching, the court of appeal to which
men turn; we live in a time when what used to be styled
"Christian civilization" or "Christian culture" has col-
lapsed. But maybe the older situation was dangerous to
the integrity of the Christian Church, tempting it to

compromise too much with the earthly, selfish aims of
nations and groups as well as individuals. Maybe it is
better for the Church to be "a remnant"—provided that it
knows its function to be that of a "saving remnant." So
the Prophet Isaiah saw the future for Israel; it would not
be dominant and dominating any longer, as a great
power, but it would be a smaller, more devoted, more
loyal, more faithful servant, suffering for the world,
offering itself in the world's service, and thus a more
suitable instrument for God's employment.

If something like this is true, as I believe it to be, the
Church's existence as the place where life in Christ is
available becomes all the more important and our recognition of its purpose all the more necessary. At the same
time it becomes even more our duty to understand that
the Church in all its various aspects is empowered by the
Holy Spirit of God. To get some understanding of what
this means, and especially what it means in respect to life
in Christ, we need to give brief consideration to the
"doctrine of the Spirit": who he is and what he does.

In the traditional theology of the Christian Church the
Holy Spirit has been regarded as "the response," divinely
inspired and indeed in itself divine, made through the
creation to God's creative and reconciling activity. Sometimes it has been put in this way: God the Father is the
Creative Source, God the Eternal Son or Word is the
Self-Expressive Activity, and God the Holy Spirit is the
Responsive Agency—there are not *three* "Gods" but there
are three subsisting and eternal modes or ways in which
God *is* and in which God *acts.* But our interest here is not
in the careful refinements of theological discussion; it is
in the practical meaning, for life in Christ, of the empowering work of the Spirit. So let us get at the matter in
a more direct fashion.

The Holy Spirit invites, incites, lures, and makes possible the response which we make in faith to what God has
done, does, and will do. Our genuinely human commit-

ment, the decision of faith, is indeed ours; but it is also
the activity of the Spirit in us. For that Spirit works
everywhere, most often secretly, to enable a response to
God's doings in the world. Once again, a very human
analogy will help us see the point. In a relationship of
deep love, the lover is moved to respond to his beloved—
Aristotle once spoke of "the power of the beloved over
the lover"—and to obey the beloved's desires, yet he
knows himself to be entirely free in doing so. In fact he
finds his highest and fullest freedom precisely in this kind
of response. The Book of Common Prayer states this
beautifully when it speaks of God "whose service is
perfect freedom."

When we choose aright, when our decisions are for the
best good of ourselves, our fellowmen, and the world, the
Holy Spirit is working in us so that we will respond to
God's calling. When we do not choose aright or decide for
the true good, we have rejected the Spirit's intimations
and lure and are held accountable for our failure or
wrong. But even then the Spirit is there, always working
to awaken, encourage, suggest, persuade, and empower
us.

To my mind we are much helped in our thinking if we
recognize that the Spirit is at work not only in human
lives and history, but also in the whole of creation. He is
active everywhere to urge on the creative process which is
the world towards its fulfilment in God according to the
level of its possibility. Unfortunately this has not always
been taught in Christian theology; there have been some
who have confined the Spirit to the specifically Christian
area and more particularly to the ecclesiastical or the
personal aspects of life. But this is to parochialize, perhaps even to trivialize, the Spirit and to make him fit into
our own neat little schemes. The scriptural view is
broader: "The Spirit of God filleth the world." Yet we
must see that at the *human* level there is, as it were, an
intensification of the Spirit's activity, because here he is

working in rational and responsible beings who can make a conscious response to what God is and does.

So, at that level, which is the level where *we* are, the Spirit *informs* our human spirit, so that we may be *conformed* to the pattern of Christ and by this conformity be strengthened to live in him as he lives in us. In the Lord Jesus Christ, God and man are so interpenetrating, so at one, that human existence is fulfilled (on the one hand) and divine reality is expressed (on the other). Those who are conformed to *that* pattern and share in *that* life are also fulfilled. To be in Christ is to be truly and fully human; it is also to express God's will and purpose on the human plane. The intention of God for man is that *as a man* (not as some angelic creature or suprahuman being) he shall represent the very quality of life which was in Christ and through Christ is conveyed to those who are his "members."

The Holy Spirit, as we have said earlier, is active in the Christian community too. He animates and empowers that community. He brings it to confess its faith in its Lord; he works in its proclamation of the gospel. Through the community's prayer, he makes the celebration of the sacraments effective. He moves the community to act in the world in accordance with its true identity. Paul spoke of "the fellowship of the Holy Spirit," in the familiar "grace" in Second Corinthians; by that phrase he meant the fellowship of the faithful which is the Body of Christ. The Spirit for Paul was the agency by whom the Body of Christ effectively became what its divine calling made it: the continuing expressive medium, through Spirit-inspired response, for the work of Christ in the world and with men.

So much for a theological introduction, although at a later stage we must return to say something more about the tri-unitarian conception of God and what this suggests about life in Christ. Let us now consider the way in which the Spirit empowers that life.

First, the Spirit works, for the most part, in anonymity. I have chosen that word with some care; what I
am indicating by it is that the Spirit does not necessarily
manifest his presence in overt or obvious ways which can
readily be recognized and named. Even in the sometimes
catastrophic moment of religious conversion, there has
been hidden preparation and there is secret lure, so that
the converted person is brought to the point where he
accepts his Lord and Saviour. Sometimes people think
that they can describe conversion by data derived from
psychological and sociological study. Such description is
interesting and has its element of truth; but it does not
fully "explain" even if it seems to "describe." For deep
down the Spirit has been at work. And in the quieter and
less exciting moments when human beings are impelled to
respond to anything good or true, righteous or loving,
beautiful or appealing, the Holy Spirit is working anon-
ymously too. He does not announce himself; he does
not make himself obvious—he maintains his anonymity,
but he is there.

This, which is true more generally, is given focal expression in life in Christ. The Spirit empowers, but we
may not always be keenly aware of what he has done and
is doing. But that does not matter, for the Spirit desires
our response rather than our giving a name to what has
made the response possible. An old friend of mine once
put this neatly: "The Spirit is humble and modest about
himself, but urgent in his action and in his demands upon
us."

Second, the ways of the Spirit's working are per-
suasive; he lures rather than coerces. He does not work so
much in spite of, or against, our desires, but by persua-
sively influencing those desires so that they are in accordance with *God's* desires for us. In other words, he
unfailingly respects the freedom which God has given us,
rather than seeking to override and demolish our freedom. Of course at some levels of the creation (where

there is inanimate matter or "low-grade" organisms) a measure of force is required to keep things in line and prevent utter chaos. But even then it is not *sheer* coercion. It is the use of force for the purposes of love—and that makes all the difference; and at our human level, this purpose of love is particularly manifest. Men may or may not accept the Spirit's promptings; he will not *make* them do so, although he will invite, suggest, solicit, and lure men to such acceptance.

Third, the work of the Spirit in respect to life in Christ is (as we have said earlier) the *informing* of men so that they may be *conformed* to the pattern of the divine will known in Christ—and conformed by their free decisions. So the Spirit works in us and upon us to structure our lives as they continue developing down the years; he patterns them towards the very likeness of Christ. Life in Christ is life in Love; hence the Spirit moves in men to bring them to the point where they respond in human love to the divine Love brought to us in the Man of Nazareth and all that he was, did, and meant. In responding they are conformed to him, the very pattern of manhood, and so become creaturely lovers, under and by means of the Love which is God and which has come to men in Christ.

A reading of the New Testament, more particularly the Acts of the Apostles, will show how this happened in the first days of the Christian community. What do we see happening there? Surely we see the awakening of an enormous movement of response to what the disciples and their converts knew of the Lord they served, and also an awakening in them of an awareness of his living presence in their midst. As they responded and as they experienced, they were conformed to that Lord's likeness. This is why it was said that "men took notice of them, that they had been with Jesus." We are impressed by the wonderful freshness and spontaneity of it all, the sheer dedication and self-giving. There was nothing forced, nothing automatic, about it. And when they spoke about what had happened, they said that in them there had been a working greater than their own human activity. This was the work of the Holy Spirit, they affirmed. Inevitably, looking back to ancient Jewish prophecy, they recalled Joel's saying that God "would pour out his Spirit upon all flesh," and they said that exactly this had now taken place. The old prophecy was being fulfilled—and the sign of its fulfilment was in the "fruit of the Spirit" seen by others in the lives of those first Christians.

Thus we have once again returned to the big theological point. God the Creative Source has disclosed himself in the world through his Self-Expression, his Son or Word; and the Holy Spirit, God-Responsive, has now moved and strengthened the "Amen" to what God has done. The life in Christ comes from God the Father; it is brought into the world in Christ who is the "en-manning" of the divine Self-Expression; and it is given its enduring strength by the Holy Spirit who brings about the response to the great event of God in Christ.

That life in Christ has both a personal and a social side, neither of which can be forgotten because in each of them the Spirit is actively engaged. On the social side, to be alive in Christ *is* to be a member of the Body of Christ and to share in Christian fellowship with other men. This is not merely human association, however. It is participation in what John calls "eternal life." The inner quality is different from the atmosphere of a club or society or school, although that atmosphere is remotely analogous— which is why some writers have spoken of the Spirit in corporate life in Christ as the community's *esprit de corps.* We have already discussed the way in which the Spirit works in the fellowship, its faith, its proclamation, its sacraments, and its outward witness. Now we need to emphasize that this *social* side is complemented by the *personal* side. The two cannot be separated from each other; they belong together and must be seen together.

When we think of the way in which the Christian as a person acts for the community in its external witness, the anonymity to which we have called attention must still be asserted of the Spirit's part in what is going on. The wonderful thing about God's way in the world is that it does not depend upon its being recognized for what it is. The philosopher Alfred North Whitehead once wrote of "the secular functions of God," and many contemporary Christian thinkers insist that God is most particularly at work in realms that we think of as worldly or secular. He does not confine himself to sanctuaries or churches. Hence life in Christ can be expressed in the ordinary activities of men in the world—in home, school, business, shop, factory, conference, planning. Yet it is also true that in what we call "religious experience," where our awareness of God is vivid in our minds, we are brought to see more clearly what it is all about and what God is really "up to" in those secular spheres. But we need to be careful lest we reduce God to our own limited ways of thinking; we must see his hand in *all* his works, secular and religious.

On the more intimately personal side, the Holy Spirit strengthens and empowers life in Christ by making more real the prayers we offer, the worship in which we engage, and the will to be disciples of Christ. More about this will be said in the next chapter; here we need only call attention to "the discipline of discipleship." The German Christian martyr of our own times, Dietrich Bonhoeffer, had much to say about this "discipline," which he even called a "secret discipline" since it is not blazoned before men. This side of Bonhoeffer's thought has been overlooked by some who eagerly emphasize what he had to say about other things, particularly about the "secular witness" to Christ in a world from which God seems often to be absent.

It is true that Bonhoeffer was insistent on Christian involvement in the "suffering of God" in the "center of the village" and not only on the "frontiers" of experience. God is to be found precisely where men live most humanly. Only so could Christian discipleship avoid triviality, futility, and frustration. But Bonhoeffer was equally insistent, even in his last "letters from prison" just before his death, that there is a Christian discipline; he called it the *arcana*, the "secret reality," in the Christian's life. He wanted to make prayer a reality for his contemporary Christian friends, but felt that much of the conventional teaching on the subject was misleading if not mistaken. He would have agreed, however, that it is not so much *we* who pray, as it is the Spirit who prays in us. The life in Christ is among other things an opening of self so that the Spirit *can* pray in us, teaching us how we are to pray. This is how we are delivered from what otherwise might seem presumptuous self-confidence in our own abilities—and the same holds true of our external conduct too, for only by recognition of the enabling Spirit can we be delivered from the idea that *we* are "doing good" in our own strength and by our own determination.

As we near the end of this chapter, it will be well to stress once more that the Spirit works where there is no clear discernment of him under his "proper name." The difference between one who lives in Christ and other men is not that the former has any monopoly on the Spirit, but that he has a glimpse of what is really going on in whatever is good, true, pure, lovely, just, and right. He can testify that his own devotion to his Lord is not by his own effort alone, although effort is required and nobody can be delivered from his human obligation to make free decisions and implement them in what he does. He can

also testify that the undergirding of his concern for social
justice and racial understanding, to take two examples, is
not merely a human desire to make it possible for people
to live healthily and happily together, but is found in the
hidden working of God, through his Spirit, towards a
shared good, in which each helps all and all help each,
and self-defeating and destructive divisions and hatred are
done away.

Paul in a great phrase tells us that "no man can call
Jesus Lord but by the Holy Spirit." And in the story of
Peter's confession of faith at Caesarea Philippi, Jesus says
that it is only by God's inspiration that his disciple has
been able to affirm, "Thou art the Messiah, the Son of
the living God." The principle enunciated in those two
sayings, of Paul and of his Master, may be given much
wider application. No man, no society, no community,
can fulfil its purpose save by the Holy Spirit, the inspiration of God. This applies *par excellence* to the life in
Christ, which includes "calling Jesus Lord" and acknowl-
edging him as "the Messiah, the Son of the living God."
Here is the reason for the frequent invocation of the
Spirit in personal prayer by Christian men and women
and in the liturgical worship of the Christian community:
"Come, Holy Ghost, our souls inspire," and "Come,
Thou Holy Spirit, come."

We seriously misunderstand these invocations if we
assume that without them the Holy Spirit would not be
present and that we must call on him to come into places
and situations where otherwise he would not be actively
at work. He is already there; he is always there, because
God is always and everywhere present and at work in his
world—as Whitehead once daringly put it, "God is in the
world or he is nowhere!" The purpose of invocation of
the Holy Spirit, as indeed of all prayer, is in the "attention" we pay to the One who is unfailingly with us. So
the early Christian writers on prayer, and Thomas
Aquinas in the Middle Ages, and John Calvin and Martin

Luther at the time of the sixteenth-century Reformation, are all agreed that prayer is "the attentive presence of God," although each of these has his own way of phrasing the fact. Prayer is always the opening of our hearts, souls, minds, and total personality, and the readiness to "hear what the Spirit has to say" to us where we are. We *attend*—we pay attention to, have regard for, are ready to accept—what God would say to us. So we invoke the Holy Spirit; and we do this with particular intent, namely that through his action now accepted consciously by us, we may respond more fully to the calling of God. We live in Christ; the Spirit aids us in deepening and strengthening that life, so that nothing in this world or out of it can shake it or demolish it: "Who can separate us from the love of Christ? Shall tribulation, or persecution, or famine, or nakedness, or peril, or sword? . . . Nay, in all these things we are more than conquerors through him that loved us. For I am persuaded that neither death, nor life, nor angels, nor principalities, nor powers, nor things present, nor things to come, nor height, nor depth, nor any other creature, shall be able to separate us from the love of God which is in Christ Jesus our Lord." So Paul wrote to the faithful in Rome, at the end of the eighth chapter of his great letter. And earlier in that chapter he had spoken of the Spirit: "For as many as are led by the Spirit of God, they are the sons of God. For ye have not received the spirit of bondage again to fear; but ye have received the Spirit of adoption, whereby we cry, Abba, Father. The Spirit himself beareth witness with our spirit, that we are the children of God; and if children, then heirs; heirs of God, and joint-heirs with Christ; if so be that we suffer with him, that we may be also glorified together."

In Christian belief the wide cosmic sweep of the Spirit's responsive work is given focus in the strengthening and empowering of life in Christ, so that we are truly enabled to live in him.

God's revelatory and reconciling work never ceases; it is what God is always "up to" in his creation. Now it has been given concentrated, intensive expression in One Man, Jesus of Nazareth, where God's activity and man's response met in decisive union. It is rather like a handclasp, in which two hands are brought together in a tight "clinch." One hand is God's outgoing Word, his Self-Expression; the other is the response of man through the Spirit of God. Always and everywhere they are coming together, but they do not remain together; the handclasp is broken. But in the one place and the One Man they are indeed "clinched." We men need to have that visibly placarded before us, so that we *know* who God is and what God does, who we are meant to be and what we are meant to do. Then we shall have the clue. We shall have something else too, that in a way is even more important for us. We shall have the power to say our own "Yes," so that what God wrought in Christ can also be wrought in us as "other Christs," in Martin Luther's (and St. Benedict of Nursia's) telling phrase.

This is what life in Christ means. Once we live in him, we are given a mission to the world. Without for a moment leaving him—for we can never leave him, since he is always with us and in us—we are sent out into the world to live and to work for God and for his glory. The Spirit enables us for this mission. Life in Christ therefore is an assimilation of our small, feeble, imperfect, sinful selves into the great, strong, perfect, and righteous One, with the intent that those selves may be used by God in love to bring his care to all his children in every time and place. By the Spirit who works within us, we who live in Christ may "do such good works as we are commanded to walk in," because we have learned, with Paul, that "to live *is* Christ"—and Christ's life is a life of humble service for the brethren.

4

The Nourishment of Life in Christ

EVERY HUMAN LIFE NEEDS NOURISHMENT OR IT WILL
faint and die. Life in Christ must also have its regular
sustenance or it too will gradually weaken and perish. In
this chapter we are to consider the spiritual food provided for those who live in Christ.

We all know that in the ordinary world not everyone
can be nourished by the same food. Each person must
have his own diet, so to speak, or at least he must find
the food which is suited to him and to his own peculiar
needs. The same is also true for those who live in Christ.
Each one has his own needs, each one his distinctive
hungers. This is but another way of saying that each of us
is himself and nobody else; each has his distinctive personal qualities and characteristics which make him in-
delibly *this* man or *this* woman. Life in Christ does not
destroy this specialty, but raises it to a higher level where
each person's talents, capacities, and potentialities may
make their contribution to the common life of men in
the family of God, the Body of Christ.

Of course the nourishment of the life in Christ is
drawn from the great store provided by the living tradition of Christian faith, worship, and life; it is not some
exotic importation from outside, consumption of which
would more than likely lead to spiritual indigestion. But
it is important to remember the variety of ways in which

this nourishment may be received into each disciple's life. The reason we should remember this is quite clear. All too often it is thought that there is for everyone a straightforward diet which he must take willy-nilly. He must accept it, precisely as it is proposed to him—three "square meals a day," and seven days a week! But the fact is that while each of us needs what might be called spiritual calories if our life in Christ, in grace, in the Spirit, is to grow healthily towards maturity, the particular ways in which we assimilate these calories may differ enormously. Or, to drop the analogy, we may remember that Baron Friedrich von Hügel, the great religious thinker and spiritual director of the first quarter of this century, was accustomed to advise those who came to him for help in their religious discipline, that they should understand and accept the quite simple fact that each man has what von Hügel styled his own particular *attrait*—that is, his own personal way of being drawn to God. He urged that nobody should try to follow the path appropriate for another although at the same time he said that there were certain given possibilities which each ought to try for himself and use as best he could. This seems to me extraordinarily wise advice. And it would be a good thing if those who attempt to help others enrich their life in Christ would grasp the implications of von Hügel's words and give their counsel accordingly.

There are three basic ingredients or provisions in the storehouse which the age-long Christian tradition offers the disciple. Each of them is good, nourishing, and helpful; but the *way* in which we use them must always be our own way and not that of somebody else. The provisions which we are discussing in this chapter have to do with the inner aspect of the life in Christ; in a later chapter we shall have something to say about the outer aspect of that life and what it both presupposes and demands.

The three basic elements which we shall now consider

are these: the practice of prayer, the use of the Scriptures, and the receiving of the Holy Communion. Mention has already been made of the three in preceding chapters, especially in our thinking about the work of the Holy Spirit in enabling the disciple to live in Christ—for it is *he* who prays in our praying, makes the Scriptures come alive in our hearts and souls and minds, and makes the Church's celebration of the sacrament effective. Now we are turning to the very practical business of how one who lives in Christ should approach each of them, with the purpose of securing from them the nourishment which he needs—although, to repeat once again the point made above, nobody can dictate just how he will do this or in just what proportions he will use the three.

There is an unfortunate idea, all too prevalent even among fairly well-instructed Christian people, that prayer is "pestering the deity for what we want"—to use a biting phrase of Dr. Inge, sometime Dean of St. Paul's Cathedral in London. It is nothing of the kind. Essentially prayer is two things: it is opening or exposing one's life to the reality of God. And in consequence of that exposure, it is aligning one's will or desire for good with the divine Love which always works for good. Everything else in prayer is contributory to, or derivative from, those two great ends. Once this is grasped by a disciple or would-be disciple, a great many of the difficulties often associated with prayer can be resolved or at least reduced to their proper proportions.

If all prayer that has gone beyond the stage of attempts to manipulate God to satisfy man's wilful desires is characterized by openness to God and readiness to align one's feeble desires with his supreme desire and purpose, *Christian* prayer has its specific quality in that it is always "in the name of Jesus Christ our Lord." The "name" of Jesus is his spirit, his very self, his disclosure of God's nature as it is and ours as it is meant to be. Thus Christian prayer is nothing other than Jesus' own prayer,

"Not my will but thine be done," in the confidence that the will of God is sheer love, sheer goodness, sheer desire for the fullest realization of that goodness and love everywhere—and in this and that specific place, too, because to say "everywhere" can be so vague that it may suggest "nowhere in particular." Thus in the life in Christ we are opening ourselves to God in those terms, in utter self-giving; we are aligning our own desires, feeble and distorted though they may be, with the desire of that love which ceaselessly and faithfully works for the good of each and of all in his creation.

To understand prayer in this way makes an enormous difference in our actual moments of praying. If we think of God in this way, how one prays and what one prays about will be vastly changed from what these might be if we thought of God in some other fashion—as an arbitrary tyrant, a dictator, a ruthless moral judge, for example. If God is taken to be passionless and static being, prayer will tend towards the *apathia* or resignation found among the ancient Stoics. If God is taken to be a moral judge and that only, our prayer will likely turn into excessive conscientious and scupulous self-rejection. If we think of God as "divine love," but by this mean only sentimentality, our prayer will be cheap and superficial and our concern for own defects minimized—after all, in the words of the French saying, "Dieu le pardonnera; c'est son métier"—"God will pardon it, that's his job"—so why should *we* bother? In that case we have a spineless attitude and our praying (also we ourselves, very likely) will be soft and flabby, cheaply and easily tolerant of wrong, not stern with ourselves as on most occasions we ought to be. And if one thinks of God's love as so austere that it lacks all passionate concern and self-giving, we shall pray with hardened hearts and doubtless become the sort of people who can only show "cold charity."

On the other hand, when the picture or model for God

is the one given in the event of Jesus Christ, he who opens his life to God and aligns his desires with God's desire will be passionate and outgoing in his concern for others, while at the same time he is inexorable in the demands made upon himself. Care for others will be combined with self-sacrifice and a certain sternness towards oneself in respect to one's failure to love as God loves.

Thus Christian prayer, while not sharply separated from the prayer of other men of goodwill who are not Christians, men who pray because (as William James once put it) "they cannot help praying," has its distinctive quality. As I have said, this is what traditional Christian language is getting at when it speaks of our prayer as "in the name, or the spirit, of Jesus Christ," and when it tells us that we should end our prayers with the words, "through Jesus Christ our Lord."

This brings to our attention another aspect of the prayer of the man who would live in Christ. It suggests to us that all our desiring in prayer—our asking and inter-ceding, for example—is to be in accord with what Paul, in Philippians, styles "the mind of Christ." Paul says that our mind should be the mind "which was also in Jesus Christ"—and that mind is then portrayed for us in the great "kenotic passage" which follows. The second chap-ter of Philippians, where all this is said, should be turned to again and again. For there Paul speaks of One who in utter humility gave himself for others, obedient to God's will "even to the death of the Cross." That is why God "exalted him and gave him the name that is above every name," so that when Jesus is named "every knee bows and every tongue confesses" that he is Lord—he has "the highest place that heaven affords" (as the hymn puts it), because his self-giving and humility are what God esteems most. Christian prayer is offered in *that* mind. It is prayer in humility and self-giving, with the desire to serve the

brethren. It is the urgent desire to do God's will because
it has been an identification of the one who prays with
that will.

Prayer, then, can be a *painful* experience, for it entails
the purification or purgation of the whole being of the
one who prays. The language which has traditionally been
used to point to this fact is for us misleading: it has
spoken of "mortification," which nowadays suggests an
invitation to masochism. But that is not the real point.
The pain or the "killing of the *selfish* self" is more like
that experienced by the mother about whom Jesus spoke;
she is in "anguish" of childbirth until she has been
delivered—and then there is sheer joy "because a man has
been born into the world." There is nothing to be said in
favor of self-torture undertaken simply for its own sake;
that is neurotic if not psychotic. There is everything to be
said for the anguish which is bound to accompany the
purging of unworthy instincts and selfish desires, so that
one can really live in Christ and find in that life the
greatest and most all-encompassing joy.

This is not the place to prescribe to the reader how he
should pray. The so-called "techniques of prayer" have
been discussed in many books which can easily be obtained. But it is absolutely essential that a Christian who
wishes to grow in grace, which is to say to live in Christ
by the Spirit and more and more enjoy the deep inner
happiness and peace which can "subsist at the heart of
endless agitation" (in some words that the poet Words-
worth used in a very different context), must engage in
prayer of this profoundly Christian type. It may be
simply turning to God each morning and evening; it may
be with words or simply with the heart's desire; it may be
for a few minutes or for a longer period of time. For
some one way is best; for others, another. All that is
demanded is that prayer be seen as an ingredient which
will nourish the life in Christ. It cannot be neglected if
that life is to be healthy, vital, and moving on towards

maturity. Prayer, as the hymn writer James Montgomery once said, is the "Christian's native breath"; without it, in some form or other, he will find that his life in Christ withers and dies.

The second ingredient in the nourishing of life in Christ is the prayerful and meditative use of the Scriptures. The Scriptures permit us to enter into the historical events which have made present experience of life in Christ a possibility for us. What might have been only the "dead past" can become for us the "living past"—indeed, a present reality—as we read and ponder the New Testament in particular. But we cannot understand the New Testament unless we have familiarity also with the Old Testament, since the latter is the account of what older writers used to call the *praeparatio evangelica*—the preparation for the gospel. As we read the Scriptures, we are aware of what has made us, and makes us, what we now are. Above all this is true in the case of the Gospels, with their account of the earthly life of Jesus. We are *there* with him, not only (as the Negro spiritual says) "when they crucified my Lord" but at other times and in other places too.

Here we have an illustration of the way in which the identity of anything in the universe, ourselves included, is established by the past which is remembered and made a living reality in our experience, the present in which we are now immersed, and the future which is our ultimate goal. The Scriptures give us the past; our day-by-day life in Christ is in the present, illuminated by the Spirit sent by Christ himself; and we look for his "coming again in glory," about which the Scriptures also speak, when he shall be recognized and accepted for what he is, Lord and Saviour of the whole world. Without some awareness of that past, which our prayerful and meditative use of the Bible provides for us, we should not know the specific quality of life in Christ. It is what he was and did, in the days of his life on earth, that establishes that specific quality. And how could we grasp the significance of the event of Christ, which thus identifies our life for what it is, unless we had deepening awareness of what prepared for his coming, what gave the context for his teaching and action, and what provided the setting for his supreme accomplishment "for us men and for our salvation"?

It is of course possible to read the Bible in a wooden and unimaginative way, with a kind of literalness which fails to see that it is the record of a continuing series of meetings with God, by a great variety of people. It can be read so that we do not grasp its significance as the record of a response made to God as he came to his people, first in the older dispensation and then in Christ, to bring them life and salvation. When the Bible is read in that way, it will have little if any value for our growth in life in Christ; it will be more like the study of a reference book or like the consulting of some divine encyclopaedia or dictionary whose chief purpose is to give us material for our theological opinions. Today, thanks to the remarkable development of biblical scholarship during the past hundred years, with new knowledge about Jewish life in its setting in the Near East, with the Dead Sea Scrolls and their capacity to illuminate the times in which Jesus lived, and much other material to which our ancestors did not have access, a Christian can use his Bible with intelligence and with imaginative understanding.

Just here is the value of the many readily available commentaries, to which we can turn for help in grasping what the "old, old story" is telling us. We can see poetry as poetry, legend as legend, myth as myth, history as history, and avoid confusing these different categories by making all these kinds of material identical. What the disciple who would nourish his life in Christ needs most of all, as he turns to the Bible, is a determination to study what is before him in a meditative way, taking it slowly, pondering what it has to say, and trying again and again to apply this to his own life as a member of Christ's

Body. For the Bible is the Church's Book—by which I mean that its context is the faithful community, which first put it down in writing and then has brought it to us through the centuries. It is normative for him, precisely because it is the record of the formative days of the Christian life in which even now he is a participant. Cold, objective, disinterested study may have its place in scholarly circles; but for the practical man the Bible is not to be approached that way. It is to be regarded as the written "Word of the living God"; and that means that it will speak directly to him. As Martin Luther said, its purpose in the Christian community is to draw him to the Christ in whom he lives; the response of faith or commitment will be awakened or deepened and the disciple will find light and life in its pages.

The Lord's Supper or Holy Communion or Eucharist is the third basic ingredient in the nourishment of life in Christ. The reason for this ought to be obvious. By our presence at and sharing in the sacrament we are brought into immediate contact with the Lord in whom we live. We may have very different ways of interpreting what happens in the Lord's Supper but we can all say with a sixteenth-century English divine that at it "our souls are happy" and we are glad that we are there.

Unfortunately many people seem to regard the Communion as a "sad" or "gloomy" service—and we must admit that some of the traditional liturgies or ways of observing it do strike a lugubrious note. But this is a great mistake. For the Eucharist, to give it its ancient name, which is the Greek for "Thanksgiving," is essentially a joyful occasion for the Christian, or ought to be. What could bring him greater joy than thus to meet with his Lord and to do this in company with others who like him are living in that Lord? How can one's mood be other than glad thanksgiving for what he was and did and above all for his willingness still to have fellowship with us in this very special and intimate way? Thus the words from an old English service should set the tone: "Let us make a joyful feast unto the Lord."

But the Lord's Supper enables us to be very realistic about this joy. For when we are present at it we cannot forget that the joy of the Christian life is not found in running away from suffering and death; it is not given us if we deny the pain that is in the world; we dare not be truly "happy" if we lose sight of the fact that it was man's wrongness which brought Christ to the Cross. How could we forget all this, when at the very center of the service is the Lord who was crucified? But we must not stop there, either. The unique Christian insight into how things really go in the world is given us when we recognize that what the hymn calls "Easter triumph, Easter joy" is also part of the story; and that we do not have a joy which is an avoidance of the wrong in the world, but a joy which finds in Easter's risen Lord the validation and vindication of his taking our wrong upon himself, identifying himself with it and with us, and yet emerging triumphant. Another of our familiar hymns has in it the phrase, "triumph in the midst of woe"; that makes the point exactly.

In the Holy Communion the Christian fellowship once more follows what by now is the familiar pattern of past, present, and future. It "remembers" the Man of Nazareth, in whom God dwelt so richly and fully, and especially his death and resurrection; it knows him in communion as a present living Lord; and it looks forward to the complete vindication (of which Easter Day is the vivid foretaste) of his life of sacrificial love. Thus the disciple is enabled to know the past now made present with a great hope for the future. Nor is this merely a "mental" experience. John Calvin wrote a small treatise on the Lord's Supper in which he spoke of the genuine presence of Christ in the communicant at that service, since by the Holy Spirit the believer is taken up into "the heavenly places" to be with Christ. This teaching has been consistently given throughout the history of the Christian tradition, whatever may have been the special interpretation of how it was brought about; it is only in comparatively recent times that some have thought that it is only in our minds that we know Christ present, as we think about him. Even the great Zwingli, the Basel reformer, who is often said to have taught such a "mentalistic" view, went far beyond any such notion.

All Christians may agree, then, that the Lord's Supper is central in their worship. It is too bad that the desire of Luther and Calvin, that the Eucharist with the proclamation of the gospel included within it should be the normal mode of Sunday worship, was not realized everywhere—largely due to reasons of a nontheological sort—and we may rejoice that increasingly their ideal is seen as the right one. It is especially interesting that the Reformed Churches, which had stressed preaching, are now coming to a more strongly "eucharistic" emphasis, while in the Catholic Church, which has put so much stress on the Eucharist, there is now a requirement that at every largely attended "Mass" a sermon shall be preached. Here is a movement from both sides which augurs well for better Christian understanding about worship.

Several times I have used the word "Eucharist" for this service; as we have seen it is from the Greek for "Thanksgiving." Nowadays many Christians are eager to speak of the "eucharistic life" as the way to understand life in Christ. This means two things. First, it insists on the importance of the Lord's Supper and frequent celebration of it as integral to the Christian fellowship's existence; hence on regular and faithful participation by the Christian disciple. But second, it insists on the life in Christ, nourished by communion at the Supper, as itself a life of *thanksgiving*. The historic background and setting of the Eucharist is in the Jewish practice of the common meal, at which bread and wine were set apart from the other food which was to be eaten and God was thanked for having given men the nourishment for their life in the world. Through gratitude and thanksgiving for God's gifts, they were able to relate everything to him and his loving generosity. So when Jesus took bread and wine at that Last Supper, he "thanked God" for them; then he gave them to his friends so that by eating and drinking with him they might share in his own life—and do this with equal gratitude and thanksgiving.

In the Book of Common Prayer there is a "general thanksgiving" in which God is thanked for "our creation, preservation, and all the blessings of this life, but above all for the redemption of the world by our Lord Jesus Christ, for the means of grace, and for the hope of glory." That sets exactly the right note for life in Christ. We who are even now being created and preserved by God are unspeakably grateful to him for all the good things he has given us to enjoy, but more than anything else we are grateful for what he has done in Christ, for the ways in which he enables us to meet him and receive his help ("the means of grace"), and for the promise of a share in his own "glory" (his manifestation of his inner self as love-in-action). It all fits together; and the Lord's Supper is one of the ways, maybe the chief way, in which this is brought home to us. This is why it is so important an ingredient in the nourishment of the life in Christ.

We have now considered prayer, the use of Scripture, and the place of the Holy Communion. For some who are reading this book, there is another helpful way of strengthening their life in Christ. They may be members of one of the traditions we commonly call "Catholic" rather than "Protestant" and they know about the possibility of a private confession of their wrong doing, wrong thinking, and wrong speaking in the presence of an ordained minister, so that they may receive from his lips the assurance of God's forgiveness of those wrongs. At one time this was thought to be a peculiarly "Catholic" practice which "Protestants" must disavow; nowadays, more and more ministers of the Protestant churches are prepared to see troubled people in what Dr. Harry Emerson Fosdick used to call "the minister's confessional," so that they may help these people find the deeply personal sense of reconciliation with God in Christ and hence reassurance in and new power for their life in Christ. The German martyr Bonhoeffer, whom we have already mentioned, urged this upon his theological students, although he told them that *any* Christian brother, ordained or not, should be ready to provide this assistance.

I shall say something about the practice here, because in our own day something of the sort seems to be badly needed by many people, whatever their nominal allegiance in denominational terms. A good way into the subject is a quotation from the English and American Prayer Books of the Episcopal or Anglican Church: "Because it is requisite, that no man should come to the Holy Communion, but with a full trust in God's mercy, and with a quiet conscience; therefore if there be any of you, who . . . cannot quiet his own conscience herein, but requireth further comfort or counsel, let him come to me, or to some other discreet and learned minister of God's Word, and open his grief; that by the ministry of God's Holy Word he may receive the benefit of absolution, together with ghostly counsel and advice, to the quieting of his conscience, and avoiding of all scruple and doubtfulness." These words are meant to be said by the minister when he is urging his flock to come more frequently and regularly to the Lord's Supper.

The invitation to those who desire it to open their hearts to a minister and receive from him the assurance of God's forgiveness and with it restoration to full and welcoming sharing in the Christian fellowship has its special value for one who would deepen his life in Christ. He *need* not avail himself of this opportunity; he *may* find it helpful to him. About this three points may be made. First, its entirely optional nature, about which I

have already written. Second, the fact that there are some
who seem unable to grasp God's forgiveness and acceptance unless it is plainly declared by somebody who can
speak with the authority of the whole Christian community. At this point I recall hearing the late Dr. Walter
Marshall Horton, distinguished Protestant theologian and
dear personal friend, tell a conference of ministers back
in the 1930's that they should be ready to hear from
their parishioners and others such an honest confession of
sin and then be ready to pronounce, in Christ's name,
that those sins were forgiven to anyone truly repentant.
Thus, he said, man's psychological need for verbalized
assurance by a minister who can speak for Christ in his
Church will be made available to troubled people who by
themselves can only agonize about their wrongness in
God's sight. And third among the points to be made, the
minister does not have any *"personal* right" to do this; it
is his privilege because he *does* act and speak for the
Christian fellowship which has ordained him. Through his
words the penitent person is enabled to know that the
fellowship, and the fellowship's living Lord, still accepts
him although he knows himself to be unworthy of such
acceptance.

Some readers may have been slightly offended by the
last few paragraphs. I can only ask that they remember
that if this particular practice is not theirs, it may very
well be most helpful to others. In any event, one thing is
clear because Jesus himself said it: before ever we have
come to repentance, God has forgiven us. It is his prior
forgiveness which awakens, or ought to awaken, our own
sorrow for our wrongdoings. The logic of God's love is
not a worldly logic, where often we must say we are
"sorry" before others will forgive us. God always forgives; and without measure. Then it is our privilege as
sharers in the life in Christ to make our glad response.

I can turn in repentance to the One who loves me, with
utter confidence in his forgiveness, because already his

"love unknown hath broken every barrier down," as the familiar hymn phrases it. Knowing this, I can make my own the refrain of each verse of that hymn, "O Lamb of God, I come." To come in repentance to God in Christ is to find renewed strength for life in him. This is the disciple's joy.

5

The Characteristics of Life in Christ

SO FAR IN THIS BOOK WE HAVE SEEN THAT LIFE IN Christ, to which every believer is called, has its basis in the historical events recorded in Scripture, in which God prepared for his special self-giving in Christ, then came in that Man of Nazareth, and thus awakened a response of faith which was made possible through the presence and power of the Holy Spirit. We have seen also that the normal situation in which life in Christ is made available is the Christian community, the Church; and we have insisted that the empowering of such life is through the Holy Spirit both in the Church and in the believer. Finally, we have seen that the basic ingredients for the nourishment of life in Christ are prayer, the meditative reading of Scripture, and the reception of the Holy Communion—and, for those who desire or need it, the possibility of a confession of faults in the presence of a minister who can pronounce with assurance that God always forgives his penitent children.

In this chapter we are to look at what I call "the characteristics of life in Christ." Since, as we have seen, the quality of that life is identical with the quality of Christ's own life in the days when he dwelt in Palestine— about which we read in the Gospels—we are also led to ask what were the characteristics of his life as we find them reflected for us in the Gospel narratives.

One place where this may be found clearly stated is in the much-loved "Hymn to Love" in the thirteenth chapter of First Corinthians, where the Apostle speaks of faith, hope, and love. Many commentators have remarked that what Paul says might well be taken as a description of Jesus himself. Jesus had enormous and confident faith in his heavenly Father; he lived in hope, both towards the Father and towards his brethren, always expecting "great things" to happen; and he lived in love of such intensity that all that Paul says about its unfailing nature is applicable to the Lord. In a later chapter we are to consider this great hymn of Paul's with this understanding of it as a portrayal of his and our Lord. For the moment it will be helpful if we use still another Pauline passage, Galatians 5:22-23.

In that passage the Apostle sums up what he calls "the fruit of the Spirit"—and it is worth observing that he writes of "fruit" in the singular, probably because he is intent upon giving a unified, harmonious account, in which we do not have a long string of moral virtues but the totality of what the Holy Spirit, working in men to empower their life in Christ, brings forth in them. Paul is telling us about the all-comprehending quality of the life in Christ when it is coming to full maturity in the experience of the believer.

The passage goes like this in the Revised Standard Version: "The fruit of the Spirit is love, joy, peace, patience, kindness, goodness, faithfulness, gentleness, self-control; against these there is no law." The last phrase, "against these there is no law," is Paul's way of telling his readers that this fruit is not contradictory to, but a fulfilment of, the Old Testament way of understanding God's will; and that it is in its own way obligatory for the Christian believer.

There seems to be some duplication in this list; nevertheless there are also subtle differences among the things named, which will make it worth our while to look at each of the terms used by the Apostle.

The first characteristic of life in Christ is *love*. How could it be otherwise, when Paul knew so well that it was God's love which had converted him, sustained him, and sought to control his very existence? That same love he saw now reflected in those whom he had converted to his Lord and for whose nurture in the Christian way he was responsible. With all their defects, they were channels for God's love and the divine love was expressing itself in their human loving. It was absolutely necessary, then, to put love first in his list; and we may add that it has been one of the tragedies of much Christian preaching and teaching that this priority has not always been observed.

We have already said much about love. Yet here we approach it from a different angle. The love to which Paul is referring, it seems from the context, is the love which ought to obtain between or among those who together acknowledge the lordship of Christ and who are fellow-members of the Christian community. It is the "love of the brethren" about which John writes in his First Letter. The first reference is to the sympathetic identification with other disciples who share in the life in Christ. But there is also what we may call an "overflow." In this instance the "overflow" is at the personal level, in terms of relationships between this and that person. G. K. Chesterton, the English essayist, once spoke of people who say they love *humanity,* which Jesus did not command, rather than their *neighbors,* which he did. Paul is talking about love to our neighbors, sometimes so much more difficult than a kind of vague sentiment of goodwill to "the whole human race." There are far too many of us who have that sentiment in a general sort of way, but who do not find it easy to love this or that particular person with whom we are in contact. Yet the love which marked the life of Christ himself was always directed to this man, this woman, this child. His love was always *personalized;* and because of this, his love made it possible for this man or woman or child to become *more* of a person.

Following upon this reference to love, Paul speaks of *joy.* This may seem surprising. Yet it must be the case because to live in Christ is always "to rejoice in the Lord," as Paul puts it elsewhere. The deep inner life of the man in Christ delivers him from a tendency to despair or hopelessness, which are the exact opposites of joy. The joy of the Christian, however, is not the superficial good cheer which disregards the pain and suffering in the world and forgets that there is much in human experience which brings anguish. Joy in the Christian sense is triumph in and through the pain, suffering, and anguish which we know so well. It becomes possible because life in Christ is anchored in the reality of God's love and therefore cannot drift into the gloomy moods which so often threaten merely human "happiness."

I am not here intending to make an utter contrast between real human "happiness" and Christian joy. There is nothing wrong with being happy. What I am urging is that the happiness we can know, humanly speaking, may be turned into the joy of life in Christ, made secure through "all the changes and chances of this mortal life," if only "our hearts are surely there fixed, where true joys are to be found." The words in quotation marks are from an ancient prayer; they put the matter very neatly, for they indicate that the supreme and all-encompassing joy of the Christian is found in his responding faith and love for God in Christ, known to us by revelation as we are empowered by the Spirit.

Next Paul mentions *peace.* Here we need to distinguish between the sort of peace which is simply absence of conflict and the deeper peace which is from God and "which passes all understanding." Certainly few things can so disintegrate human life, both personally and socially, as warfare within or without. Conflict, when it is not the positive tension which can be creative of further good, is a terrible and devastating experience. The peace to which Paul refers is grounded in the security offered us by our faith in Christ; it can endure in the midst of the agitations in the world about us as well as the inner struggle to decide for what is truly good. Whatever happens to us, the love of God in Christ will never let us down, never desert us; and in every aspect of life "God is working towards a good end for those who love him," as Paul says in Romans 8:28. Such a certitude is the meaning of peace.

Even in those times when the disciple feels himself "forsaken," he can remember that his Lord knew that same experience on the Cross ("My God, my God, why hast thou forsaken me?") and yet came through to peace because he was sure of his Father's never-failing love and care which would never let him go. Indeed the very fact that Jesus began his "cry of dereliction" with the words "My God, my God," and that he followed that cry by saying "Father, into thy hands I commit my spirit," indicate that there was in him an inner security about his mission and its safety in God's hands. His life as a Man was "hid in God," even in the trial and suffering he had to endure. The disciple's life is also hid, but now "with *Christ* in God"; and *with Christ,* because from Christ he can know the reality of a peace which the world can never take away, because the world did not give it in the first place—*God* gives it, God only.

The peace of the Christian is this inward assurance; it is also expressed outwardly, for he is to be "at peace with the brethren," and with all men everywhere. This is true too of the next characteristic the Apostle notes: *patience* or long-suffering. Internally and externally, patience is the acceptance of the necessity for waiting and the expectation that good will appear. In its root meaning the word "patience" is related to two ideas: experience and suffering. Both are relevant here. The man who is patient is the one who "puts up with" what he must experience in life. At the same time he is confident that some good will emerge, even if it is not the exact good which he might have wished to appear. Despite our human pride, none of us can make the world over as he might choose. Our decisions have their result, to be sure, and we can do something in our human freedom to bring the future into conformity with its intended direction to fulfilment; but we cannot prescribe what is to take place—if we try to do so, we shall be most bitterly disappointed. But the patient man has his *hope,* which is set on the good that is God's purpose working itself out in the creation and in his own life. Thus patience is both acceptance of the present for what it is and also a hope for the future, in whose realization we will have our part, under God's supreme controlling wisdom.

Here again the life in Christ is a reflection or re-presentation of the spirit in which Christ himself lived. He was patient, accepting others as they were and accepting above all God's will for himself. He was patient in enduring the uncertainties and even the apparent defeats which faced him, "running with patience the race that was set before him." He was utterly confident that God's will would be done; and he knew that his own vocation was to be the agent in the accomplishment of that will, cost what it might. So, in their own way, with those who live in him. They are able to accept and to endure, having come to know how things really go in God's world—and having been given the grace to distinguish between "what can be changed" and "what cannot be changed," as Reinhold Niebuhr once put it. They are patient in doing what they are called upon to do; and patient with others who do not always respond quickly, readily grasp their possibilities, or act responsibly.

Thus to be patient is not always easy; it is a matter of training and experience. It "takes time," we might say. But the impatient man, constantly striving and continually irritated by what happens to him, is not really living in Christ—or, to phrase it a little better, he is not fully alive to the possibilities open to the one who lives in Christ. His very impatience is a sign that he is not moving towards full maturity in his Lord.

Next in Paul's list is *kindness.* We need to be careful lest this kindness should be taken to mean only being nice to other people. Obviously it is right to be kind to others. Human life would be a great deal more pleasant, and human society a great deal more satisfactory, if more people were kind to one another. But the kindness about which the Apostle is writing is much more positive than that. He is talking about goodness or love *in action,* the going out of oneself to surround others with the deep concern which will enable them to be their best and to realize, as fully as is possible for them, the potentiality they have to become genuinely mature personalities. This sort of kindness has its "cutting-edge"; it may be expressed best, not by easy toleration of what is wrong, but by bold witness to what is right. No man is truly kind when he lets a friend slide slowly into evil ways, without bringing to bear upon him his affectionate concern for his doing better than that. How we witness to this concern is a matter which requires thoughtfulness and understanding. There can be no question of imposing on the other our own notions of his true good, against his will or by a presumptuous claim that we always know best. Perhaps most often the effective way to be kind to another is by just being with him in his worries and troubles, in his moments of anxiety or anguish as he must make important decisions, and in his wrestling with the responsibilities that are his. And when someone else is happy, we can be with him too, sharing his joy and letting him see, more by what we are than by what we happen to say or do, that we care deeply for him and rejoice with him. It need hardly be pointed out that Jesus was like this; therefore the life which is in him will be like this too.

That is how goodness works; and *goodness* is next in

Paul's listing of the "fruit of the Spirit." Goodness is a moral virtue, of course; as such it is an active interest in, and doing for, other persons in the affairs of life. But it is also an inner principle; and maybe it might best be defined as integration of personality. The good man or woman is one who can be counted on to do his best in any circumstances and for anybody he meets. This surely is a reflection of Jesus' own attitude and conduct; and in him it sprang from the inner principle of an integrated human personality whose center was in God and his loving will. Only through a right relationship with the cosmic source of all goodness, God himself, is there the possibility of goodness like that in human existence. The inner reality manifests itself in the outward acts, which are good acts because their source ultimately is in him who is altogether good. They will also be kind acts, for they will be acts (or thoughts or words) which have consideration for other persons and for their development to full manhood.

Now we come to *faithfulness*. Life in Christ by its very definition is faithful life, since it is commitment to God disclosed in the event from which that life takes its origin. Faithfulness means dedication of self, or engagement of self, in the other or others to whom the self is related. First of all, in the life in Christ, that dedication is to the Lord himself; then by derivation it is to one's own sure purpose of growth in this life; and finally it is faithfulness or dedication to the good of others. The faithful man is unswervingly loyal to what he believes; in his action he does not waver in witness to that loyalty. We know how this can happen in our ordinary human experience. To be faithful to a friend is to be loyal to him because one *believes in him*. And when we say that a husband is faithful to his wife, we mean more than that he is not guilty of adultery with another woman; we mean that he believes in his wife, cares for her, and in all his relationships with her is dedicated to her best good.

The French novelist Albert Camus has a story about "a

woman taken in adultery." In her case it was not a matter
of engaging in sexual relationships with a man who was
not her husband; it was that she dedicated herself to, and
found satisfaction in, a seascape which struck her as
unusually beautiful. So Camus would tell us that faithfulness demands a commitment to another which is such
that no person or thing can take the place of that partner
in thought or in deed. To be sure, this is a hard saying. It
is so hard that few of us can attain to its demands all the
time and without many lapses. Yet surely it is one of the
greatest and most rewarding of human possibilities.

Jesus was thus utterly faithful, both to his heavenly
Father and to those whom he met and knew. The Gospel
stories make this very clear. And the man who lives in
Christ reflects this same quality in the integrity of his
character and in all he does.

The next item in Paul's list is *gentleness*. The opposite
of gentleness is brusqueness, harshness, arrogance—all of
them most unpleasant qualities. The gentle person, on the
other hand, is not assertive of self, nor harsh and disagree-
able in his relationships; he does not act arrogantly but
acts in a spirit of comprehension and sympathy. He need
not be "soft," although cynics seem to assume that
softness and gentleness go together. The truth is very
different. The person who is truly gentle is the person
who is truly *strong*. He is "safe" in his inner life and
direction and therefore he does not need to assert himself
arrogantly as a compensation for inner insecurity and
uncertainty. Those who try to lord it over others are
usually those who are very unsure about themselves. So
the depth psychologists have told us, with great insight
drawn from their experience of counseling, that most
frequently the sharp, harsh, domineering man or woman
is in his "insides" a frightened person whose only way of
finding some safety is in external severity towards other
people.

If I agree at once with somebody's ideas or accept

without question whatever he says to me, I am not being gentle; I am being weak and pusillanimous. But if I express my own convictions in a sympathetic and friendly way, I am not in the dreadful position of attempting to dominate my acquaintance. Gentleness in this sense includes a witness to one's deepest beliefs and a refusal to let another easily succumb to a second or third best when a first was available. But the gentle person knows well enough that he too may be in error since he is not in possession of all the facts of any person's life. That is why he will not push, shove, drive, or coerce. Instead he will relate himself to the other, in openness and friendly sympathy but with real firmness, hoping that the other may be brought through this attitude to think more deeply about the matter in question.

The Lord was like that. He was gentle but he was strong. So too must be the man who would live in Christ; he will be hard on himself but gentle with others. He will not try to control them or "boss them around," but will live with them in understanding and deeply sympathetic awareness of their problems and concerns, whatever they may be.

Last in Paul's list comes *self-control.* "Temperance," used in the Authorized Version to translate Paul's word here, is not adequate to the Apostle's meaning, since the word today has a somewhat negative suggestion. What Paul is getting at may be put in two ways. First there is the sort of integrity of personality about which we have already spoken. The man who is in control of himself, in the Christian sense, is the man who has given the control of his life to the One to whom rightly it belongs: to God himself. Self-control does not mean the "Uriah Heep mentality," as it has been called, in which we invite others to trample on us; it does not mean sheer killing of all one's human desires, wishes, aspirations, and hopes. That is as far from true "self-control" as it is from the humility which is also characteristic of life in Christ. The point is rather that since the disciple's life is centered in God's love in Christ, in whom his human self has found its point of reference, he will be unfailingly obedient to that truer self which has replaced the "selfish self" which is so much the victim of cheap and wrong inclinations and tendencies.

The second point about self-control is what the word "temperance" in the Authorized Version signified at the time when that translation was made; our modern English would speak here of "moderation." Aristotle wrote in the *Nichomachean Ethics* that a rule of good conduct was "Nothing too much." Yes, in a way this is true. But the trouble here is that Aristotle's "magnanimous" or "great-souled" man seems to be far too much a cold, calculating person, self-contained and unwilling to take great risks. In this sense his suggestion of a *via media*—not too much of this, nor of that, but a middle road between them—can be deadly and horrible. It can destroy spontaneity because it is afraid of going to extremes.

On the other hand, we can learn much from an ancient Christian view, in fact based on some things said by the same Greek philosopher, that during one's life a *habitus* or habitual way of thinking, relating oneself to others and governing one's own life, may be built up. Thus by God's grace we may develop the *habitus* of living in accordance with God's purpose of good as disclosed in Christ. This will not destroy the spontaneity of our actions; it will simply give them a direction which is always followed, whatever may be the particular decision or deed in this or that instance. In fact, one of the significant aspects of life in Christ is such a gradual adoption of that kind of direction, which enables the disciple to deal with instinct, desire, and drive in a fashion that will be for his, and for others', best good—precisely because it is the *God-given* direction which always aims towards love and goodness "in widest commonalty shared." That is how Christ himself lived; that is how those who live in him may live.

The good things of this world are not to be despised, for they are God's gifts, his creation, and by that very fact good in themselves. It is how we use them that may often, if not always, be *wrong*. Desire is not to be suppressed simply because it is human; it is to be given the proper sort of expression. As John Calvin, and before him Augustine, rightly saw, man is indeed "corrupted" in every area of his life; but the corruption is not *total.* Calvin's phrase about corruption has been misunderstood when it has been interpreted that way; what he meant was that no element or part of human existence is without some wrongness, not that man is rightly defined as "just a total mess." Hence we need to let the Holy Spirit align our desires, and everything else about us, with the perfect good that is God revealed in Christ. Then we can see the truth of Augustine's great saying that if once we love (and he meant that we love God as the supremely lovable), then we can do "what we like." This is both moderation *and* spontaneity. It is not "lawlessness" but obedience to what Aquinas called "the new law in our hearts" which is "the love of God."

In the last paragraph or two we have been speaking about "direction." This brings us to the final comment in this chapter about characteristics of the life in Christ. What matters most is not whether the Christian has "arrived." Of course he has not. But it matters supremely that he should be going in the right direction. Life in Christ is a life which is growing, maturing, developing. It is on the move. It is energetic and vital, not content to stop at some point along the way and assume that everything has been accomplished. We are to "press on towards the goal of the mark of our high calling." We are to "grow up in every way into Christ . . . to the attaining of mature manhood, the measure of the stature of the fullness of Christ."

6

The Enemies of Life in Christ

THERE IS A STORY ABOUT AN OLD AND DEVOUT CHRIS-
tian who was asked by a Salvation Army lassie if he had
"found peace." He answered, "No, my dear. Not peace
but constant struggle." Of course the fact was that he *had*
found peace, of the sort about which in the last chapter
we were speaking; but the point which he was making
was that in a very real sense the Christian life is indeed a
"constant struggle." To live in Christ is not to be "at ease
in Zion"; it demands continuous warfare against the
enemies of that life. In this chapter we shall consider
these enemies, against which every disciple must be on his
guard and which frequently he must fight with all his
strength.

Once again we turn to Paul's letter to the Galatians for
help in our discussion. In that epistle, just before he lists
the various qualities which are the "fruit of the Spirit,"
he speaks of the enemies of that Spirit and then lists
some of them: "Immorality, impurity, licentiousness,
idolatry, sorcery, enmity, strife, jealousy, anger, selfishness, dissension, party spirit, envy, drunkenness, carousing, and such like" (Galatians 5:19-21). Obviously he is
just writing them down as they occur to him; equally
obviously, it is possible for us to arrange them in a
somewhat different order and then to see that there are

seven enemies, some of them with one or two or three special aspects, which deserve our careful consideration.

I have arranged them in the following way, with the particular heading for each group: immorality (including impurity and licentiousness), idolatry (including sorcery), wrath (including enmity, strife, and anger), jealousy (including envy), selfishness (which in all its horror must stand by itself), needless controversy (or dissension, and "party spirit"), and lack of self-control (including drunkenness and what Paul calls "carousing"). These are all enemies of the life in Christ; they are the attitudes and actions, or states of mind and feeling, which militate against that life, preventing its growth and doing great damage at the stage in his growth which the Christian has already reached.

As in the last chapter we shall think of each group *seriatim.*

First, then, there is *immorality.* As we all know, Paul lived and worked in the Graeco-Roman world of his time; and as a pious Jew in background and morality he was deeply shocked by the moral laxity, especially in sexual matters, which he found in so many parts of that world. In Corinth, for example, the situation was such that the very name of the city had become a symbol of sexual vice; the name had been made into a verb to indicate what we might well call "shameless licentiousness." To "corinthisize" was to behave in an utterly immoral way with no regard for standards of conduct that commended themselves to the thoughtful and decent citizen of the Roman Empire of the time.

The Jewish attitude towards human sexuality was very different from anything found in that great commercial city. The Jews did not take a negative attitude to sex; they regarded it as a good thing because it was part of God's creation and they never showed the moral negativism that has sometimes been found in Christian communities. At the same time, however, they were strict in observing a high standard of sexual behavior, whatever may have been the lapses of individuals. As a Jew Paul had been brought up according to that high standard. When he touches on immorality in this passage and elsewhere in his letters he is not to be understood as denying sexual instincts or condemning them as evil. Unfortunately some people have so interpreted him, taking a few of his more violent reactions against the prevalent licentiousness as the basis for this interpretation. In understanding what he was saying, we need always to remember that the details of his teaching on sexual matters come much more from his own Jewish tradition and background than anything else. Indeed, on occasion he makes it clear that it is *he,* not the Lord, who is speaking. Thus there is a certain relativity in our interpretation of his teaching, just because he was never thinking of laying down a set of requirements for the centuries which were to follow.

But one point is very clear about Paul's attitude here. He is sure that man's body, like his soul, ultimately belongs to *God;* and as a Christian he is sure that the man who lives in Christ must not fall into sexual libertinism, for this is one of the serious enemies of the life in grace and in the Spirit. Quite apart from the Apostle's particular slant on the matter, anyone can see that a person whose sexual life is not ultimately under what we may well call "control by love" (by which we mean the deepest concern for another as equally with him the child of God) dissipates his sexual energies and deprives himself, as well as others, of the possibility of true growth towards a full and complete life. The very word "dissipate" is instructive, for its dictionary meaning is "scatter without regard for consequences." This helps us see why the Christian tradition has put such stress on chastity, although (alas) too many have used that word in a purely negative sense. The English Quaker philosopher John

Macmurray has done us all a service when he suggests that the true meaning of "chastity" is "emotional sincerity." In putting it that way, he says positively what Paul is saying negatively. The opposite of "immorality, impurity, and licentiousness" is not the denial of man's sexual desires, instincts, and drives, but "emotional sincerity" in the use or expression of them. As the Danish thinker Søren Kierkegaard so beautifully told us, "Purity of heart is to will one thing"—and the one thing willed is the love which is of God, from God, and blessed by God.

We very much need a popularly written treatment of what might be styled "the Christian doctrine of sex." If I may be immodest, I tried to do this in a very preliminary way in a book *Making Sexuality Human* (United Church Press, 1970); it was nothing but what I have called it, *preliminary,* yet it has been encouraging to hear from dozens of people who have read it that it has suggested to them a positive, yet controlled, approach to their sexual life. However that may be, it is clear that once the love of God in Christ Jesus our Lord is at the heart of a man's life, so that he is beginning to live in Christ, this love must be reflected in a control of sexual, as of all other, desires and drives. "Willing one thing" and "emotional sincerity" will be dominant. Then cheap sexual promiscuity, sexual vulgarity, and all the rest of those manifestations that can be so unpleasant, will be ruled out. Sexual behavior will be a visible disclosure of what a man is "in his heart"; for what he is *there* is shown in how he treats others, not least in the area of sexual relationships.

One final comment must be made. While immorality, in this sense of sexual license, is an enemy of life in Christ, it is also true—and frighteningly so—that Jesus himself seems to have been more troubled about "the cold sins" than about sins of passion. It was hypocrisy, malice, covetousness, contempt of others, and the like which received his greatest condemnation. These are even worse enemies of the life in him than the sexual misconduct which is so much more obvious to our eyes. Thus a Christian disciple will imitate his Lord in saying that the person guilty of sexual license is not to be hated or rejected, although what he has done has been very wrong and frightfully damaging to his possibilities for growth in Christ.

Next in our grouping comes *idolatry*. The background for the Apostle's thinking here is to be found in the prevalent worship of what he called "false gods" in the Graeco-Roman world and along with it the practice of witchcraft and divination (or sorcery). Perhaps the latter is not so remote as we might like to think from our contemporary situation, since many who have lost Christian faith have turned to various sorts of spiritualistic, astrological, or even quasi-magical practices, the use of charms or "mascots," and other strange kinds of superstition. But the former, idolatry, is very much with us, although the forms it takes are often highly sophisticated. Men do not bow down to "idols of wood and stone" nowadays, but they worship idols perhaps even more false and certainly more dangerous to their inner life: success, wealth, respectability, political power, national pride, and the like. To be set free from the worship of these idols is a great liberation—and it may be worth saying that the contempt which so many modern young people show for such idols often adored by an older generation is altogether to their credit, even if their way of making this clear is not always pleasant.

In the life in Christ, there is no room for anything which can pretend to take the place of utter loyalty to God as disclosed in Jesus Christ. To put anything in that place is to deny the disciple's profession of faith: it is impossible to serve God in Christ *and* anything else which makes a false claim to our dedication and service. In one sense all these idols, like the ones made of wood and stone in an earlier day, are ready-to-hand, easy to worship, and make no demands on ultimate loyalty—or if they do, they hide this under the veil of some pretended good. Yet in another sense they are all-demanding and hard to worship, since they take what there is of a man, distort his life, and prevent his growth in grace.

The Christian has but *one* Lord, "him whom God has sent" to disclose his love and to reconcile us to himself. A familiar hymn by William Cowper prays that the Christian may be strengthened to "tear from his heart" all such idols and give his rightful place to Christ. This demands an assiduous discipline so that there will be no chance for anything else to occupy the throne. Of course there are good things in life, perfectly right ambitions, entirely good concerns; these are to be used or sought. Yet Augustine made an important point when he took two Latin words and applied them to this matter: *frui* and *uti.* He said that we are to use (*uti*) these goods of the world but not to rest in them as if they were absolute goods; we are to give ourselves in sheer delight (*frui*) to God only and to nothing else whatsoever. Where perhaps he misled us was in his failing to see, or at least to say, that much of the time the supreme good is known to us through the immediate available goods. Because that is so, we must seek the highest or supreme good which is in and behind all the good things of this world, without contemptuously dismissing as bad what God has created. And finally only the *summum bonum,* that supreme good which is really God himself, has the right to the absolute allegiance of the man who is living in Christ.

Our third group is *wrath,* which includes anger, enmity, and strife. Anger is obviously a bad thing, except when it is "righteous anger"—outrage at cruelty, pretense, contempt, and all manner of evil things. But the more subtle form of wrath, shown in the spirit of enmity, is even more dangerous than an explosion of temper. At least temper is warm; enmity is bitter and cold and can hurt much more than an outburst which may last for but a moment. The man who is always looking for occasions to condemn and destroy is a dreadful person. He poisons his own life and the lives of others. "Storm and strife" do not go together with the quietness of the spirit, the inner peace, which in our last chapter we saw to be characteristic of life in Christ. They are a denial of that quietness and peace; and they show clearly that their victim has not gone very far towards maturity in his Christian discipleship.

There is one area of experience where a good deal of control can be exercised over what we call "temper." I can say this because I myself have had to learn to suppress a tendency to express moods of irritation that could hurt others. But the danger of "suppression" is that it will only drive the trouble deeper into oneself, where it will fester and poison one's life. That is why the only really effective way to handle this, and other sorts of anger and annoyance, is to "fall in love." That may seem to some an odd way of putting it, but I mean this very seriously. To fall in love with what is good and true and lovely, whether this be God himself or one of God's "surrogates" who stands for him (*not* a substitute, which takes his place), will channel the aggressive tendencies that are behind anger, enmity, irritation, and wrath, into attacks on what is really wrong, evil, false, ugly, and hateful. This provides what William James once called "the moral equivalent of war." And this is why a faithful commitment to God in Christ can bring into our lives the quality of positive goodness which marked the days of Jesus in Palestine. We are invited to fight with God, and on God's behalf, against all that is inimical to the truest good of his creation.

This makes it clear that a Christian is not meant to be a weakling nor to act like Mr. Micawber, always expecting something good "to turn up" but never doing anything to bring it about. The Christian's indignation is against sin, not the sinner; the wrong, not the wrongdoer; the evil, not the fellowman who acts in an evil fashion. He will not confuse the wrong done with the person or persons who have done it. If he did he could not get into a relationship with them which might be of help. Jesus drove the money-changers out of the Temple; there is no evidence that he was angry with the men as human beings—it was their mistaken, misguided, wrong business that provoked his righteous indignation. His attitude was always on the positive level; even in his vigorous condemnation of Pharisaism and the Pharisees as a group, we do not hear that he showed wrath at this or that particular Pharisee. On the contrary, as we see in his way of treating "Simon the Pharisee," he sought to reason with them and bring them to a better mind. And on the Cross, when he might have lashed out at those who had condemned him and were mistreating him, he prayed, "Father, forgive them, for they know not what they do." In that same spirit, received through his continuing relationship with his Lord, the man in Christ will not strive with others, nor be angry with them, nor despise them, nor be their enemy. His will be a positive, not a negative, attitude.

We come now to *jealousy,* with which we have linked envy. Jealousy, the "green-eyed monster," is one of the worst enemies of life in Christ. A grudging attitude, unreadiness to accept the fact that others are more gifted or have more possessions or occupy a better position than I do, refusal to concede to somebody else what he has achieved or earned: this is what Paul is talking about. The opposite is of course generosity of spirit; and the man who truly loves, because he is caught up into life in Christ, cannot be other than generous. He knows that he has himself been loved more than he deserves; he has been accepted although he knows himself utterly unacceptable. How then can he fail to love others? How can he fail to accept others, although they may have what he would like or what he may think he has deserved?

Basically jealousy and envy are a manifestation of what classical theologians have always called the root sin,

namely pride. Although in this list Paul does not mention
it, he knew well enough that it was man's worst enemy
and the supreme opponent of life in Christ. For pride is
placing oneself at the center of the universe, whereas the
universe has but one center, God. A man who is so wrong
about this will inevitably be jealous of others, envious of
them, because they threaten his own supposed self-
sufficiency. Their talents, possessions, position are constantly before him as a commentary on his own imperfection and inadequacy. But life in Christ is open, generous,
accepting of others, and can even rejoice in their good
fortune. Why? Because the man who lives in Love can
only live in love. He will be stern with himself, see
himself for what he is, put God where he belongs—at the
very center of things—and be content if he can sense even
the slightest movement forward in his path towards
maturity in Christ.

Next in our list we have *selfishness*. When we speak of
this, which in a way is the most horrible and deceitful of
all our enemies, we need to make a careful distinction.
For there is a kind of concern for self which is right and
sound. Jesus himself implied as much when he told us
that we were to love our neighbors *as ourselves*. He did
not want his disciples and followers to *kill* their selves,
but to lose those selves in loving concern so that they
might find them again, purified, purged, ennobled, and
enriched. Unhappily some writers on Christian themes
seem to have forgotten this altogether when they suggest
that the self is the root of all evil and must be destroyed
before men can be saved. What they should have said was
that the "selfish self" is in need of drastic treatment.
After all, to exist at all requires some concern for the self,
both physiologically and psychologically. Where things go
wrong is when the self is so much at the center that
nobody and nothing else counts at all. In this sense
selfishness is almost another name for pride.

A poem by the American Rolfe Humphries speaks of

hell as the place where the only word ever spoken is "I, I, I." Egocentricity like that is indeed appalling. It leads to the attempt to lord it over others, to insist upon our own righteousness and rightness, to act and think and speak as if we were "masters of all we survey." And it is all based upon a vicious lie, for as we said above the only center of the universe is God. He alone could "lord it over others," although in his loving care he never seeks to do this. He alone is righteous and right. He alone is the "master of all he surveys," although in his mastery he does not coerce and force but persuades and lures, entices and invites, his creatures to accept his sovereign rule because that is not so much for his own greater glory as it is for their greater good.

The man who lives in Christ is not egocentric; he is theocentric—it is God who is at the heart of things, not himself. Christ is his master, and he is the disciple or follower and not the lord. Above all, he is deeply immersed in love; and love casts out selfishness of that sort, just as it casts out fear. God's purpose for us is not that we deny our manhood or our being selves, but that by putting first things first we realize our true manhood and our true selves. So the man in Christ is on the way to true fulfilment of selfhood, which is the opposite of egocentricity.

Now we come to needless *controversy*—to dissension and what Paul calls the "party spirit." Perhaps we can best think of this enemy of life in Christ as a contentious spirit, in this respect not too far from some aspects of the wrath or anger we have already mentioned. The man who is contentious need not be overtly angry; his inner mood in itself is bad enough. When he is present, there is a feeling of dis-ease or discomfort. This can in the end bring chaos to a community, while it is disastrous for the man himself because he is in a state of rancor. So also the partisan, with his fixity of outlook and unwillingness to learn from others, sows disharmony wherever he goes except among those who happen to share his prejudices. And his own attitude prevents his thinking rationally and clearly, in fairness to those who disagree with him.

Within the Church, such people are not infrequent; certainly the polemical type of professing Christian, especially the one who holds his position without any generosity of spirit, is responsible for much that is unattractive in the life of the organized community. Religious controversy is the most unpleasant of all controversies—and especially unpleasant when those who engage in it are themselves "good men." Pascal says that men never sin so cheerfully as when they do it with a good conscience; and often enough religious polemic is conducted by those whose conscience *is* good—that is why they can, if not cheerfully then certainly zealously, speak and act as they do. A friend once said that there are people who do not engage in thought but simply in the "rearrangement of their prejudices." They adopt an unyielding attitude because they simply will not listen to criticism nor open their minds to truth which they have not themselves arrived at. This attitude is destructive of real understanding among men.

All this is bad enough for the common life. What concerns us especially is that it is also damaging to the personal life of the man in Christ. What it can do to him is to narrow, even embitter, his spirit so that it is absolutely impossible for him to grow towards that maturity in Christ which is expressed in openness, readiness to learn, and delight in sharing with others, whether Christian or not, in their experience of life in the Lord. The love which so marked the Lord's days in Palestine, and which life in him is to re-present, cannot flourish in such an atmosphere of controversy, dissent, contention, and partisan spirit.

Finally we must speak of the lack of *self-control* at which Paul is pointing when he writes about "drunkenness and carousing." Here too we have to do with serious enemies of life in Christ.

Doubtless in the Apostle's own day "carousing" meant mere gratification of the senses, mere seeking of momentary pleasure, whether through excessive consumption of wine or through participation in careless and cheap satisfactions. Drunkenness would be related to this, since under the influence of strong drink men can become uncontrolled and uncontrollable, offending others and damaging themselves. Surely neither of these is unknown to us today in a society which often seems to be intent only on pleasure, however obtained. Nowadays we might wish to include the use of drugs which artificially stimulate while in fact they harm the addict.

But the main point to be stressed is that *any* lack of self-control, whatever the way in which it expresses itself, is a way of dethroning Christ and in his place substituting readily available and superficial satisfactions which even pagan writers have recognized as harmful to man's best development. The Christian must avoid all such. To repeat what has been said before, however, this does not mean a denial of God's creation nor of the proper use of the good things that God provides for men in that creation. Nor does it suggest that a Christian is to be a "kill-joy" who because he really *hates* that creation cannot bear the sight of other men having a "good time." He cannot be a sadist, who inflicts pain; neither can he be a masochist, who delights in being hurt. Once more he is controlled by the love which is from God through Christ; and that will make all the difference in attitude and in act.

These are some of the serious enemies of the life in Christ; and a Christian must be aware of them and struggle against them. Or, to put it in a better way, he must so open himself to the very life which lives in him, Christ's own life, that *it* (or *he,* for it is Christ himself) can vanquish these enemies and bring the disciple farther along the road to full maturity.

Farther along the road, yes; but again we need to remember that it is not so much *arrival* which matters as movement in the right direction. Full arrival is hardly to be expected. We shall fall victim time and again to one or other of the enemies of Christ. And we shall do this for at least three reasons. First, there is the frustration of living in a finite and limited world to which most men from time to time feel themselves ill-adjusted and against which they react with some measure of violence; second, there is the long accumulation of wrong decisions throughout history, into which we enter and by which we are inevitably influenced in making our own decisions for good or for ill; and third, we find it so much easier to choose the obvious, immediately available, and superficially attractive alternatives. Traditional theology has summed these three up in a single phrase, "original sin." The phrase is not an entirely happy one, but the reality to which it points is plain enough. Man as he is now is not able to live, act, choose, in the way which is really proper to his God-created nature; he has gone, and he continues to go, astray—and the Greek word *hamartia,* which the New Testament uses for sin, itself means "wandering from the way" or "missing the mark."

Granted this, however, it is the direction we are taking in our life in Christ that is important. We cannot judge others, and in one sense we ought not to judge ourselves, by the particular point of achievement of good or commission of wrong that we know at this or that moment in our lives. Indeed it is only *God* "unto whom all hearts are open, all desires known, and from whom no secrets are hid"; he is the One who can make a just appraisal of our situation and that of others. But if we somehow sense that we are "on the way," moving towards "ripeness in Christ," we can take heart.

Thus the disciple knows that his Lord will be faithful; hence, "I know whom I have believed and am persuaded that he is able to keep that which I have committed unto him . . . ." The beginnings of life in Christ are in us. We cannot rest in our own efforts, imperfect and often wrong; we must use the "spiritual weapons," about which the Epistle to the Ephesians tells us, as we combat the enemies of that life. But Christ, God in Christ, is at our side and within us; and we can go on in the assurance that we are always loved, accepted, and cared for.

7

Faith, Hope, and Love in the Life in Christ

THE THIRTEENTH CHAPTER OF FIRST CORINTHIANS IS doubtless the best known of all biblical passages, except perhaps for the Twenty-third Psalm in the Old Testament and the Parable of the Prodigal Son in the New. The chapter has been called Paul's "Hymn to Love," for it is a celebration of love and its expression in human life. So familiar is it that for many it is simply taken for granted. That is why I shall now give it in full, in the Revised Standard Version, with the last few verses of the preceding chapter which provide its setting. Reading it again will give point to what we shall be saying in what follows.

"Now you are the body of Christ and individually members of it. And God has appointed in the church first apostles, second prophets, third teachers, then workers of miracles, then healers, helpers, administrators, speakers in various kinds of tongues. Are all apostles? Are all prophets? Are all teachers? Do all work miracles? Do all possess gifts of healing? Do all speak with tongues? Do all interpret? But earnestly desire the higher gifts.

"I will show you a still more excellent way:

"If I speak in the tongues of men and of angels, but have not love, I am a noisy gong or a clanging cymbal. And if I have prophetic powers, and understand all mysteries and all knowledge, and if I have faith, so as to remove mountains, but have not love, I am nothing. If I give away all I have, and if I deliver my body to be burned, but have not love, I gain nothing.

"Love is patient and kind; love is not jealous or boastful; it is not arrogant or rude. Love does not insist on its own way; it is not irritable or resentful; it does not rejoice at wrong, but rejoices in the right. Love bears all things, believes all things, hopes all things, endures all things.

"Love never ends. As for prophecies, they will pass away; as for tongues, they will cease; as for knowledge, it will pass away. For our knowledge is imperfect and our prophecy is imperfect; but when the perfect comes, the imperfect will pass away. When I was a child, I spoke like a child, I thought like a child, I reasoned like a child; when I became a man, I gave up childish ways. For now we see in a mirror dimly, but then face to face. Now I know in part; then I shall understand fully, even as I have been fully understood. So faith, hope, love abide, these three; but the greatest of these is love."

When the thirteenth chapter is taken in connection with the last verses of the preceding one, as we have just done, we can see that the Apostle was speaking specifically to those who were "the body of Christ and individually members of it." That is to say, he was speaking to those who live in Christ, since to him membership in the Body and life in Christ are identical. His purpose, therefore, is to indicate the quality of life which should mark every man who is in Christ—whatever his office or work may be, in the community itself (to which he makes specific reference) or outside it. None of these offices, none of this work, constitutes in itself "the more excellent way." The jobs done and offices held are important for him, of course; but his point is that every Christian, whether in some "official" post or not, is called to the "more excellent way" which is the way of love, although faith and hope are intimately and inextricably associated with love.

In an earlier chapter we noted that some commentators have said that in the account Paul gives of love and its working through faith and hope, he is in fact describing Jesus himself. From what the Apostle knew of the Lord through the tradition which he had received and from his own experience of his risen Master, he can paint him in a word-picture. Certainly this suggestion is interesting, perhaps true. Jesus was "patient and kind," never "jealous or boastful," nor "arrogant or rude." He did not "insist on his own way," nor was he "irritable or resentful." He did not "rejoice at wrong, but rejoiced in the right." He "bore all things, believed all things, hoped all things, endured all things." His love "never ended." Even if the identification of love as depicted in I Corinthians 13 with the earthly life of Jesus may be open to scholarly doubt by some, there can be no question that the Apostle is speaking most certainly about what in his own experience of the living Christ he knew well. And although Paul never minimized the earthly life of Jesus, whom probably he had never seen, nor thought that life unimportant for his own faith, it is plain that the center of his existence was in the living presence and power of the Lord. Thus one might say that in this celebrated passage he is speaking primarily of the Christ in whom he lived, the One who for him was the visible expression, the very image, of God's love towards his children.

Since this is the case, we have every right to interpret the passage as also describing what it means for any Christian to live in Christ. And because the origin and foundation of life in Christ is in the events associated with the name Jesus, the events of which Jesus was himself the focus, we have the further right to relate what is said about this present existence in the risen Lord with the Man who "went about doing good . . . for God was with him." Unlike some of the ancient "mystery religions," with their worship of a heavenly lord, the Christian way puts its emphasis on the identity of the earthly Master and the present exalted Lord. It re-presents both, for both are one and the same. The Christian has been grasped by the historical *and* present Christ in such a way that the quality of Jesus' earthly life comes alive in him, as he is in fellowship with the risen One. What Paul says about love may therefore be taken to refer to the historic Jesus who is also the living Christ and to the life in Christ which the Apostle said was the whole significance of being a Christian.

Much has been written about Paul's doctrine of redemption or salvation or reconciliation through Christ— his soteriology, to use the technical theological term. This has been so strongly, and rightly, emphasized, that there is a danger of our forgetting another aspect of his thought. What the famous German historian and doctor Albert Schweitzer used to call "the Christ-mysticism of Paul" must not be overlooked. Another famous German New Testament scholar, Adolf Deissmann, wrote a learned book on that very subject; and even if one dislikes the phrase which both of these men used, the fact to which it points certainly requires no demonstration for anyone who has carefully studied the whole body of Pauline writing and does not give attention only to the numerous passages in which the Apostle explicitly writes about sin, redemption from sin through Christ, and the "justification" (or acceptance of man) which God effected in the death and resurrection of the Saviour.

For our purpose in this book, we must not overlook for a moment the "saving work" of Christ but we must see it in intimate relationship with the Pauline teaching about life in Christ, membership in the Christian community which is the Body of Christ, and the work of the Holy Spirit in making possible growth in grace for the one who has been "brought out of darkness into Christ's glorious light" and thus enabled to share in "the glorious liberty of the children of God." This is the practical consequence, in our vital Christian experience, of what God has wrought in his Son.

In the last two chapters we have examined some of the characteristics of life in Christ and we have looked at some of the enemies of that life. Now we are to focus our attention on faith, hope, and love. We shall think of each of these from three different angles. First we shall consider them as marking the life of Jesus himself as he is portrayed for us in the narratives in the Gospels. Then we shall consider them as marks of the life of the disciple who lives in his Lord. Finally we shall rather daringly consider them as characteristics of the life of God himself. I say "rather daringly" because such an attribution of faith, hope, and love to God the sovereign ruler of all things is by no means common among theologians, some of whom might regard such an attribution as bordering on blasphemy. This rejection would certainly be made by the theologians who maintain a conception of God which puts its final emphasis on what traditionally has been called "the divine *aseity*" or self-existence and self-containedness, the absolute being of God apart from all his relations with his world, and his sheer impassibility or inability to know or experience suffering in any form. But for those who like the writer would put the primary stress and the final emphasis on God's love and his participation in the world and human life, seeing his other attributes as adjectives qualifying the way in which that love is and expresses itself, the situation is quite different. For them, an attribution of faith, hope, and love to God seems required for a sound theology. Nor is this a "reduced" theology, either; in terms of the biblical witness and of Christian experience, it is (so we think) the only possible theology and the highest theology possible for us to accept.

So we turn first to the earthly life of Jesus.

The total impression conveyed by the stories about

Jesus in the Gospels is plain enough, whatever some may think to be the problems associated with the details in the telling. Here was One who had unquestioned and unquestioning faith in God, whom he called "Father" and whose will was for him the guiding principle in all that he said or did. "My meat is to do the will of him that sent me," John represents Jesus as saying; and the total record leaves us in no uncertainty that this was indeed the case. If faith is to be understood as commitment, Jesus was an entirely committed Man. Furthermore, his whole hope was centered in the inexhaustible capacity of God to effect his purposes in the world; and this hope was no wistful desire but a strong and eager expectation of the great things God would do. The Gospel narratives are marked by what scholars call an "eschatological note": that is, there is throughout them a constant looking towards "the last days," when God will establish his Kingdom in the world. Whatever Jesus may have thought about his own place in the Kingdom whose advent he proclaimed, for him that Kingdom was to be *God's,* in which his own place would be found; and all of his efforts were directed to preparing others to look for, expect, hope for the coming of the great day. His death can only be understood in terms of that faith and hope. He gave himself up to death, "even the death of the Cross," in utter commitment to his heavenly Father and in the strong expectation (or hope) that God would use his self-offering for the accomplishment of his purpose, and towards the bringing in of the Kingdom.

Certainly nobody can fail to see in the Gospel stories the reality of the love which God had for his Father. Just how Jesus understood his relationship to the Father has been much discussed among New Testament scholars, but none of them can deny the fact of the relationship as portrayed in all the records we possess. We cannot engage in a psychological study of Jesus' consciousness, for the material in the Gospels was never intended to make him the hero of a psychological novel. While this prevents us from indulging in a "psychograph" (as the American historian Gamaliel Bradford used to do with the persons about whom he wrote), it does not call in question the patent reality of his total turning of personality in love towards God, nor his urgent loving desire to do always the Father's will.

If this is true in respect to Jesus and God, it is equally true in respect to his relationship with his disciples and with others whom he met. Faith in other men was as real as faith in God. This is why Jesus could always make an immediate contact with them, for it is only one who believes in another person and in his hidden possibilities who can awaken a response of trust and commitment. "Deep speaks to deep"; and because Jesus was always prepared to commit himself trustingly to those whom he met and sought to help, he himself was received by them in reciprocal commitment and dedication. This is the way in which the One who proclaimed God's Kingdom as his gospel became himself the object of men's faith. So it was that the message preached by Jesus could become the message about Jesus; that is the logic of the development of Christian faith in its very earliest days. It is odd that some New Testament scholars have not seen this point and have drawn a far too sharp distinction between the gospel Jesus himself preached and the gospel that within a very short time was preached about him. They have been too intent upon some theological model of their own to take due account of simple facts, both in the New Testament record and in the ordinary experience of men. The initial commitment of the disciples to Jesus was their response to his faith in them; and the simple "man in the street" can readily see how this would happen.

Jesus also had hope in others. This hope was no wistful idea that they might be better people someday; it was an eager and urgent expectation that from the very depths of their being would emerge a response which would make them more truly men. Hence in his contacts with others he appealed to the latent possibilities that were present but so often obscured and unrealized. Jesus "knew what was in man"; and this means that he knew not only what John in his Gospel intends when he says this, where the implication is probably the evil hidden in the human heart, but means also the remarkable capacity of the Lord to see good where others did not or could not see it. The story of the tax collector is an illustration. Jesus saw more in him than an avaricious exploiter of others. So also he saw more in the woman taken in adultery than the others present, who thought of her simply as a sinner. Jesus saw in her a possibility for goodness and true love; he treated her accordingly.

The cynical suggestion has been made that there should be another "beatitude": "Blessed [should it not be "cursed"?] are those who expect nothing, for they shall not be disappointed." When a man feels that nobody has hope in him, he is likely to sink into lethargy and not bother; when he knows that someone does have "great expectations" from him, something is awakened in his heart so that he strives to come up to what is expected of him. In any event, there is always more in a man than meets the eye. There are all sorts of hidden potentialities, planted there by God himself. What is needed is the sun and rain which friendly hope can provide, so that those seeds may come to fruition. In Jesus' relations with the lonely, the outcast, the sinners, the forgotten, and the despairing, the sick in body and mind, his very hope for them evoked something which nobody could have thought present—except the One who cared enough to hope.

Even more obvious is Jesus' love for all sorts and conditions, all types and classes, of men. Where the Gospel narratives do not spell this out, it is obvious to the careful reader. "Actions speak louder than words"; and in Jesus' actions his inner attitude revealed itself over and over again. The way he treated others—that same tax collector, for instance, the arrogant Pharisee, the woman "who was a sinner," the despised "people of the land" who could not manage to keep all the minute rules laid down by the Pharisees, not to speak of his own immediate disciples and others with whom he was in contact in his itinerant preaching—manifested in concrete action his care for them, his interest in them, his desire to help them, and his willingness to give his time and his energy for them. His love for men was shown above all in his final act, when he died for men so that in God's Kingdom they might have life.

Jesus' faith, hope, and love for his heavenly Father were the motivating power for his faith, hope, and love for his fellowmen. So we must say that if Jesus is indeed (what so many modern writers tell us) "the Man for others," he could be this because first of all he was "the Man for God." He could be like that for men because he had committed himself to God, expected great things from God, and loved God above all else. So in respect to men his faith, hope, and love were made an inexhaustible and unwearying reality. Those who have no such motivation from a relationship with the Source of all love and goodness and strength are all too likely to become weary in well-doing, disappointed because of the slight response they receive in so many instances, and hence prone to give up when "the going gets hard" and the return is not obvious. It has been said that there are many many "tired liberals" who have stopped struggling for men's freedom and justice because they have too often encountered serious obstacles to their effort. There are also the men of genuine goodwill, the humanistic secularists of our day, who become impatient, even irritated, when their good offices are rejected. But with Jesus it was different. Because he had faith, hope, and love towards God, he could continue in faith, hope, and love towards men, come what might and disappointing as the results might seem on the surface of things.

If Jesus was like this, the Christian disciple who lives in him is meant to be what I have styled a re-presentation of this quality. So we come to our second main concern: how faith, hope, and love are seen in life in Christ. Towards God, known in Christ as the great Lover of men, the Christian will have faith and hope and love. He will commit himself utterly to God as Christ has revealed him; he will expect the great things which God has prepared for his children; and he will love the Lover who cares for him and for the whole creation. Likewise, the man who lives in Christ will commit himself daringly and openly to other people, prepared for the risks that this involves. He will expect great things from them, knowing full well their present inadequacy but knowing also that God is at work in the depths of their being. He will love them, giving himself in care and concern, accepting them "just as they are" without demanding that they shall first show themselves worthy of his acceptance.

At this point we need not elaborate further, since most of what might be said has already been stated or implied in earlier chapters. The man in Christ will not have arrived at his Master's perfection; in his weakness and wrong he cannot. But the direction of his life is right. More and more, often in ways that are anything but obvious, he is growing towards true maturity in ·"the knowledge and love of God and of Christ Jesus his Son." Hence he is growing in faith, hope, and love towards God and towards the brethren. The latter include those within the community of faith, with whom he is in intimate relationship; they include also those outside the Church, who nonetheless are God's children and his own brothers. Christ died for them all; and the man who is in Christ is called to give himself for them too.

And now we come to our third main concern in this

chapter. I have called this a "daring" application to God
of the faith, hope, and love which were manifested in
Jesus' life and are the secret reality of the disciple's life
too. God, the supreme divine reality who is at the very
center of things and whom we worship and adore, is also
the One who has faith, hope, and love. Can we really
speak of God in that way?

We cannot speak of him thus, if we think of him as the
absolute and immutable First Cause who exists in separation from his world. Such a God would not be open to
his creation, suffering with it and rejoicing with it. Of
course we might say *in word* that he is loving, yet that
love would be a sort of benevolence, rather than the
passionate outgoing love which seeks to share, identify,
and constantly be present with the world and men. Such
a God could not be at all affected by what happens in the
world. He would know it, yes; but it would not enter into
his own being so that he would sorrow over wrong and
delight in good. For some of us, that "model" of God,
however conventional it is and however much it has been
regarded as highly orthodox, is the worst of all heresies; it
is even apostasy from what Alfred North Whitehead was
accustomed to style "the Galilean vision" of God's nature
and his action in the world. We may even say, with
considerable boldness, that all too often Christian
thinkers—but not so often simple practicing Christian
believers—have substituted for that "vision" of God as
"pure unbounded love" (in the words of Wesley's hymn)
some idol, whether it is the idol of "imperial Caesar," the
earthly despot now made heavenly, the "ruthless moral-
ist" become a heavenly dictator, or a static Absolute who
ultimately "could not care less" about what goes on in
his creation. But the specifically *Christian* "model" for
God is no abstract reality nor tyrannical emperor nor
frightening moral dictator, but a *Man:* the Man of Nazareth, in his courageous love, his illimitable faith, and his
unsuppressible hope.

Working with such a "model," as surely a Christian must, we can see how it is entirely appropriate to attribute to God those three qualities seen in Jesus: faith, hope, and love. To refuse to make such an attribution would be to fail to think of, and relate ourselves to, God in terms of the One whom Christians call his incarnate Son; it would be to set up an idol in place of the true and only God.

The tragedy of it all is that in our own time many good people, including some of our most thoughtful contemporaries, are in such violent reaction to those idols—sheer power, moral ruthlessness, unconcerned absolute being—that they have been prepared to deny God altogether. They have been led wrongly to assume that such conceptions of God are the truly orthodox ones, whereas they are (as I have just tried to show) appallingly heretical and apostate. But because these people have been misled, they act as if there were no God at all; some of the more intellectual of them have gone to the lengths of declaring that "God is dead." It is not *God* who is dead; it is those false pictures of him. People like that may be blamed for their failure to distinguish between "models" *that have died on them* and a genuine rejection of the true and living God whom those idols have so badly misrepresented. Yet, I think, the ultimate blame must rest, not on the men who have spoken and written in this way, but on the false or misleading teaching which has led them to think as they do.

So let us dare to say that *God* has faith in his world and in his human children who live in that world. He commits himself in utter self-identification with the world and his children—if he did not, what would the Incarnation and Atonement signify? Yet it is not only in Jesus Christ that God thus commits himself to the world; he is doing it all the time and the presence and action of God in Jesus are the clue to what God *always is*, what God is *always up to*. We must not pay God what someone

has called "the metaphysical compliment" of thinking we
exalt him when we think of him as utterly removed from,
or unidentified with, or uncommitted to, his creation.
For in the event of Christ he discloses himself with
singular intensity as identified and committed. He has
faith in the world he is continually creating; he has faith
in what may be achieved in that world from which he is
never absent.

So also with hope. God hopes for his world. Since it is
he who knows all hearts, all desires, and all possibilities,
he sees what the poet Gerard Manley Hopkins so beautifully called "the dearest freshness deep down things."
How could he not, since it is he who has put that
"freshness" there? His concern is to bring it to open
expression. Expecting great things from his creation, he
gives himself to bring them about; through his Spirit
active in it, he awakens a response which many would
have thought impossible. His expectation brings about
the great things that he expects. We can twist that "beatitude" about the man who expects nothing and make it
now say, "Blessed be God who expects great things, for
he cannot be disappointed." Despite all that is wrong in
the creation through its many false choices, despite man's
sinfulness, despite the frustration which finite conditions
impose, despite any and every factor which works against
hope, there is always the possibility of realization of
good. God knows this; he appeals to this; he employs
this—and the good does happen.

When it comes to God's love for his world and for
men, we need add nothing to what has already been said.
"His nature and his name is Love," said Wesley; because
that is true his attitude and action in creation is always
and everywhere loving. There is plenty that is wrong
about the creation; we are not to be silly optimists. But
God's love is greater than those wrongs. It is unwearying
and cannot ultimately suffer defeat. So of God, who
identifies himself with and shares in his world even to the

point of anguish, it may be said (in words which Isaiah applied to God's Suffering Servant) that "he shall see of the travail of his soul, and be satisfied." The final end of it all will be triumph and joy in Love's victory.

As we close this chapter, let it be noted that there is a remarkable interrelationship between faith, hope, and love in Jesus' life, those things in the life of the man who is in Christ, and those same things in the very heart of God himself. This is a threefold reality—a threefold cord which cannot be broken, as an Old Testament text puts it. Our life in Christ has its origin and foundation in the event of Christ and all that it signifies; but it has its deeper origin in the God who worked through that event to reconcile the world to himself, to accomplish his purpose of making men his conscious and personalized agents. Life *in* Christ is the life *of* Christ; and the life of *Christ* is the life of *God* made humanly visible in him. It is "eternal life"; it is "life indeed."

8

The Fruits of Life in Christ

IN THE LAST THREE CHAPTERS WE HAVE SPOKEN ABOUT
the characteristics of the life in Christ and the enemies of
that life, and then of the great illumination thrown on it
by the Pauline triad of faith, hope, and love. Throughout,
our primary interest has been in the inner life of the
Christian disciple. This was right; and for two reasons.

First of all, and very practically, in this day of mass
movements, great organizations, and so much else that
stresses social matters, there is a danger that the interior
life of men may be forgotten. Indeed there has been a
considerable shift in recent years, not least on the part of
younger people, from emphasis on the big, impressive,
organized side of life, towards a renewed awareness of the
need for nourishment of man's deep personal self. Hence
the strange interest in eastern methods of meditation, in
exotic spiritual cults, and the like. In a way it is a sad
comment on the failure of the established Christian community to provide help here, that people have felt obliged
to look outside the tradition of Christian faith to find
help in this matter. And one of the reasons for writing
this book is to make clear that while, as we have so
frequently insisted, membership in the fellowship is
necessary for full Christian discipleship, the life in Christ
finds a special focus in this and that particular person and
in his spiritual condition.

The other reason for our treatment in preceding chapters is the simple fact, of which Jesus spoke so plainly, that it is *from the heart,* from the inner man, that his motivation for external or outward Christian expression must come. Furthermore, without that deep inner reality it is all too likely that his outward acts will be frenetic, disordered, or (as a friend once put it) "reeking of the spur of the moment."

But it is now time to turn our attention to what I have called in the title of this chapter "the fruits of life in Christ." Note that here it is "fruits" in the plural, not (as in an earlier chapter) the "fruit" produced by the Spirit in men as they live in Christ. We are going to think about the many different external manifestations, in all their variety, of that inner life "hid with Christ in God" which is the secret reality of life in Christ.

Before we begin this discussion, however, it may be well to return to some points made in the two opening paragraphs. Much of the frustration and sterility felt by so many today, I believe, accompanied as it often is by a despair about accomplishing anything towards making a better world, rests primarily on the long-continued neglect of the "inner man." When Christianity is simply identified, without remainder, with "going about doing good," it may be reduced to a good deal of going about; and that is all. Then there is an emptiness about life because there is no reality which fills life with the peace and harmony within, whose product is thoughtful, consistent, and devoted action. There is a connection between what goes on inside a man and what he does in external conduct. Certainly the Christian disciple has his base in the life with Christ; his outward acts are the "overflow"— as was suggested in an earlier chapter—of that rich and abundant life which Jesus came to give and which he will unfailingly supply to those who turn to him.

Nevertheless the outward acts are of enormous importance. And Jesus himself was insistent on that importance. He taught that men must live in love and charity with their brethren, that they must seek the common good, and that they have an obligation to do works of mercy—in a word, that there is a social dimension to the life lived in him. Jesus gave himself for others; so must we.

Three preliminary comments must be made here. First, it is necessary to see that Christian activity is not the same as "busyness." Many of us have known people who in their zeal have consumed their energies and wasted their strength in an indiscriminate running-around, with (for example) continual attendance at meetings and faithful pursuit of good causes. The end-product has been that when they were presented with a real opportunity to act constructively in a concrete situation they had no strength, no energy, left; their enthusiasm had been dissipated in futile activism.

The second comment is equally simple. Christian action is not thoughtless and unplanned. In saying this I do not suggest that everything must be "systematized" and that there is no place for spontaneity. My earlier remarks in this book should have made that obvious. But it is useful to point out that one of the aspects of human nature is rationality, with the possibility of making plans. The Christian, like everybody else, will be wise if he follows the advice Jesus gave in his parable of the man who went to war without considering his possibilities of winning. To order one's activity in such a way that the maximum use may be made of the resources available is simply human wisdom. But it is divine wisdom too, as Jesus said. Without some such planning, there is the possibility (perhaps the certainty) that one will spread himself all over the scene, with no depth of penetration at any point and hence with little accomplished in the long run.

The third preliminary comment may seem the exact opposite of what has just been said; but it is not. I refer now to what I have called the spontaneity of the Christian in action. Spontaneity is *not* thoughtlessness or acting on immediate impulse. If it were that, it would be a harmful and dangerous thing. But true spontaneity is a certain freshness, a readiness to respond to unexpected situations for which exact details cannot be worked out, and a genuine openness and eagerness which will deliver one from simple routines for their own sake into a meaningful activity towards a valuable end. The spontaneous person is not somebody who "breaks out everywhere"; rather he is the enthusiastic, keen, interested, and energetic person who is prepared to act wherever he can be genuinely helpful.

Our major concern in this chapter is with those areas of external Christian action which desperately need the Christian witness and in which that witness can most effectively be brought to bear. I am thinking of matters like race relations, social justice, overcoming the barriers imposed by class or other artificial human distinctions, international understanding, and similar questions. In these areas Christians of necessity have an interest; in each and all of them their participation can be useful, while the fact of its being a definitely *Christian* participation will have its own special significance. For it is bringing the love of God in Christ Jesus to bear upon problems that threaten to destroy our world. It is a testimony to the fact that there is *reality* in the life in Christ, so great that it affects everything a man does and thinks and says in the ordinary places of life and in the big issues that confront the world.

A faith which does not somehow express itself in these ways may rightly be called irrelevant; it may even be a dead faith. A hope which does not express itself is no longer eager expectation but a cowardly refusal to be involved. And a love which does not find ways of loving in the world at large is likely to be little more than pious sentimentality. So also a life in Christ which does not reach beyond itself—like the goodness of God which classical theology always rightly described as *diffusivum sui,* expressing itself by necessity of its own nature as good—and does not concern itself with the neighbor, the city, the nation, and the world, is twisted in upon itself and can become a poisonous rather than healthy and health-giving cell in the total human organism. Indeed, it is not life in Christ at all, but a cheap imitation. And like all imitations, sooner or later it will be shown up for what it is—or, more accurately, for what it is *not.*

It ought not to need saying, yet unfortunately it does, that becoming a Christian should make a difference. For far too long and among far too many people, Christian profession has been looked upon as a sort of veneer applied to the surface of things, to give them a shiny finish. It has been something added on to the ordinary ways of human behavior, rather than something which changes every aspect of that behavior. Altogether too many people have thought that attending church services from time to time, so they could be listed in the census as a member of this or that Christian denomination and look with some disfavor on others who claimed no such allegiance, was what it meant to be a Christian. This is not so much the case as it was a half-century ago, for nowadays it is possible to be accepted as a decent and upright member of society without ever darkening the doors of a church, with no profession (real or pretended) of Christian belief, and even with a certain contempt for Christian ideals. Perhaps the change is all to the good, if it can awaken Christian people to the truth that by what they do they bear witness to what they are; that what they believe in their hearts they must show forth in their lives. It makes a difference when one becomes a Christian, when one shares in Christ's life. If it does not make this difference in outward acts as well as in inward condition, there is something very seriously the matter. Surely we should all agree that this is true. If we do not, it would be more honest simply to stop calling ourselves Christian.

The Christian does not reject the world nor does he attempt to run away from the ordinary responsibilities of daily life. In a striking passage in one of his books, Søren Kierkegaard (the great Danish Christian thinker and writer of the last century, whom we have already quoted in this book) said that the "knight of faith"—his name for the faithful Christian disciple—will probably appear to his contemporaries to be in almost every respect simply another citizen. He does his daily work, he enjoys his times of recreation, he likes to be with his family and friends. As Kierkegaard quaintly phrased it, he walks in the Deer Park outside Copenhagen looking forward to his Sunday dinner at home and those who see him do not think of him as an "odd man out." Yet in a very deep sense he is just that. For the inner motivations which are his and which govern his ways of thinking, speaking, and acting, are not those of "the ordinary decent chap." They come from his inner life in relationship with God in Christ. And when there is need, or when some crisis comes, or when there is an appeal made to him to help another, or when he sees a wrong which he can do something to right, or when he comes across a cause that needs support, his inner life expresses itself in outward acts. It cannot help doing so, since the Christian has been more and more sensitized to the world as God's world, where God wills that men shall be his agents in righteousness—a righteousness which in fact is nothing other than love in action. Then the difference between him and others becomes very plain indeed.

The American preacher Theodore Parker Ferris, in his little book *Facing West,* has written these words: "When you are young, you begin by loving life, and you want to draw it all into yourself; and that is right and normal. But as you grow older, there ought to be a discriminating refinement, weeding out this and that which has proved less valuable than other more durable things, until finally, instead of wanting to draw all life to yourself, you want above everything else to give what life you have to others. Living will then mean Christ to you, more and more. And the other things will not be eliminated; they will be subordinated to that one central desire."

That is beautifully said; and Dr. Ferris is right. He is really doing nothing but describing growth in Christ and the way in which that growth naturally leads a Christian to "want above everything else to give what life he has to others." There is the deep motivation about which Kierkegaard was writing, which differentiates the disciple from others. His concern for justice, peace, sharing, understanding, and the rest is very real indeed. But maybe that of other men is too. *His* reasons are not theirs, however; and that means that when he does act, there will be some subtle quality about his action which will redeem it from cold calculation, from simply human concerns for the right and the good, and will be felt and seen by others who, sometimes without quite knowing what they are observing, cannot help "taking notice of him that he has been with Jesus." Or, if they do not think or say that—for they may know and care nothing about Jesus—there will yet be visible before them something which they are bound to feel is just a little special.

Now no Christian could think that by his concern and work for social justice, say, he is bringing in God's Kingdom. Certainly he urgently yearns that God's kingly rule may be known on earth as it is in heaven. But no human effort will "build God's Kingdom" in the world. That Kingdom is God's to give, when he will. Yet there *is* something a Christian can and must do: "prepare and make ready the way" for the Kingdom and work to bring men and women everywhere to the point where they can be aroused to their responsibilities, however they describe them in words, and can recognize their need for acceptance and love. The Christian is one who lives in Christ, as a member of the Body of Christ; he knows the enabling power of the Holy Spirit. Hence he orders his own life, and would do all he can to order the ways of the world at large, so that all is in readiness for God's love to be manifested at any moment and in any place in the long process of human history in which this love is being expressed, and can be accepted, known, and enjoyed in all its reconciling and fulfilling power.

There is nothing automatic about this, since love does not work according to a timetable or like some mathematic equation. Yet in "preparing and making ready the way" for the advent of love here, there, in that place, at that time—which can be anywhere and everywhere, as T. S. Eliot says in one of his poems—the disciple is a "fellow-worker" with God—or in Whitehead's fine and bold phrase, "a co-creator with God." The reign of Love, which is God's Kingdom, may come at any time. We represent this to ourselves—or to phrase it more accurately, the gospel message represents it to us—by the wonderful picture of the future advent of the Kingdom, glimpsed and anticipated here and now ("The Kingdom of God is upon you," said Jesus), but in its full reality still to come. And that coming may be sudden and quite unexpected, as happens to the man or woman who, as we say, "falls in love" without any previous notion that this is to happen. Or the coming may be more gradual and imperceptible, as can also happen to a man or woman who through the years discovers himself slowly brought to love another, without catastrophic moments but in a steady growth in affection. But however and whenever that sovereign rule of God as love enters history or human experience, the point for the Christian disciple is his having shared in preparation for its reception, acceptance, and the working out of its implications in the here and now.

Thus he is indeed a "fellow-worker" or a "co-creator" with God. But so are all men, or at least such is the divine

intention for all men. How then does the man who lives
in Christ differ from them? What *is* that difference about
which we spoke some pages back? Surely it is in this:
First, the Christian is confident that through no merit of
his own he has been given the clue to what creation is all
about, where it is getting, why it is there at all. This he
has received through the reality of Christ in whom he, as
a disciple, "lives and moves and has his being." The
meaning of the creation, in every aspect, is that it is the
field or sphere in which the divine Love is at work,
ceaselessly active to bring it to its fulfilment by delivering
it from all evil and wrong and by enabling it to realize (or
make real) the hidden potentialities which he has placed
in it. In a word, the Christian knows God as Love,
revealed in Christ, active in the world, purposing great
things for that world.

And second, the Christian is recipient of the enormous
energy of the divine Love—theologians call this "grace"—
which has been released in Christ; he participates in that
Love as he lives in the One who is Love incarnate and
redemptive. Thus he has both the vision to see and the
power to work for the *real* good which God wills for his
children.

Obviously the Christian still sees "through a glass,
darkly"; he does not know the whole truth, as God
knows it. There is a vast area about which he must remain
ignorant, which indeed no man could ever know. For
God is a mystery; so also, in a derivative way, is the
creation. Yet the man in Christ can say, without pride in
this knowledge since it is a gift to him and not a matter
of his own achievement, that he has learned how the
world goes, where it is going, and why it is going that
way. This has come to him through the total event of
Jesus Christ, where it has been disclosed in an act which
is so vivid, so striking, that it has evoked a response never
before seen in history. The disciple is caught up into that

response: he lives in faith, by grace, through the Spirit of God.

Now that certainly makes him different.

We have spoken of such issues as race relations, social justice, and international understanding; and we have said that the Christian must bear his witness and take his place in the solution of these problems. I have mentioned these matters of great social importance because all too often Christian men and women are unwilling to do just this. Here it is not possible to discuss the ramifications, the details, the many subsidiary questions, which these and similar problems pose for the Christian, as for any other genuinely concerned citizen. My point is simply that a Christian cannot subtract himself from involvement just because there are difficulties and because he may run the danger of "sticking his neck out." He can claim no technical competence in handling most of them, unless it happens that one or another area is his particular special secular concern. Nor can he say that there is only *one* way, which presumably he knows, for handling the matters. Not only his charity but his common sense ought to make that impossible.

One of the interesting signs of the times is the renewed awareness of this wider social dimension on the part of Christians who in many traditions have hitherto been unwilling to see their responsibility there. The very fact that these Christians, for the most part from evangelical groups, have a firm basis in Christian experience of life in Christ, will give them a place to start, a point of view, and a type of approach which will deliver them from making too pretentious claims for themselves and their ideas. Certainly we must hope so, since a defect in some other groups' participation has been a rather overweening confidence in themselves and in the rightness of their opinions about what can and should be done in these and other areas of great moment.

We have observed that "love of the brethren" in John's
First Letter seems to be specifically directed towards
those who share in the life in Christ in the Christian
fellowship—the "in-group," as contemporary sociologists
would put it. But it would be a grave mistake to think
that this exhausted love's expression. God's love, we
insisted, is diffusive. It cannot be confined to any single
community at all, not even the fellowship of the Holy
Spirit which is the Church; it must spread itself and make
itself known in all the relationships of life. Thus it is
possible to bring John's teaching to bear upon the more
general external expressions of life in Christ. It is the
same love, now overflowing into every aspect of human
existence and working to make things over into the
pattern of God's purpose for that existence. Love of this
urgent sort is no theoretical goodwill, any more than it is
pious sentiment; it is passionate devotion to God's will,
deep concern for all men, and a dedication of self to God
and to them. .

John tells us in the fourth chapter of his letter that a
Christian is to "test the spirits," to see whether they are
truly "of God." His meaning is that all the causes to
which the disciple is invited to give himself are to be
placed alongside the "coming of Jesus Christ in the
flesh"—that is, alongside the disclosure of God as "pure
unbounded love" in action in the world. So he can
determine whether or not these causes are worthy of
Christian dedication. In the immediate situation to which
he was writing, the author was thinking of the so-called
"gnostics" who were the followers of a teacher named
Cerinthus. They evidently held to a version of Christianity, but did *not* take with sufficient seriousness the
concrete historical "en-manment" of God in Jesus Christ.
Hence John condemned their views, urging that Christian
faith is centered in that concrete fact. What John said
there we can apply more widely to anything that would
command our service. It is to be appraised in terms of its

capacity to provide a place for and opportunity of expressing God's love, whose innermost quality is made known in Jesus "come in the flesh."

Having set forth this criterion, the writer tells us that God *is* Love, known to be such not through intellectual speculation but through his having acted in Christ. The love which we feel rising up in our hearts is not merely a human affair; it is God's own love for his world, working in us and through us in the world. Its human side is not denied, for John never rejects the world and human life; on the other hand, that human side is taken up, purified, and used by God. And because "God so loved us," we "also ought to love one another." There is no room for dissension, partisan spirit, or the other "spirits" which fight against Christ; by the Spirit "whom he has given us" we can live in love with our brethren and defeat those enemies. The love we show is first of all to our brethren in the faith; then it flows over into love for all men, whoever and wherever they are.

And then he makes a daring statement. "No man has ever seen God," he says. Yet "when we love one another," the love which we then experience is really nothing but the love which is God himself, coming to us in and through human love. When we "live in love" we "live in God" who *is* Love. To know this, to experience this, to express this, is to see that God is not far from us, because it is "in love" (which is to say also, in Love—to use once again the upper-case letter to show that we speak of God) that human life finds its truth, completion, fulfilment, and goal—in God himself.

John goes on to say that when a man truly loves, he is delivered from the fear which so often dogs his existence as a man. He is given the "confidence," which all so desperately need, that this existence of his is not futile and that he is not simply the victim of circumstance. Nothing so inhibits meaningful action as the anxiety which arises from lack of confidence and the fear that in what we do we are necessarily in the wrong or are doing the right thing in a wrong way. All this is done away, John tells us, because "there is no fear in love, but perfect love casteth out fear." And he relates this to the dread day when we shall be appraised for what we are. The man who knows such love as this need not fear the judgment, since already he has been accepted in love by the One who judges and the appraisal to be made will be in terms of complete understanding and deep concern.

Thus the disciple who lives in Christ has been liberated. He is now free from all that could prevent his acting in the world bravely, courageously, and gladly, as the personal instrument for the Love which is so much greater than himself. The love with which he responds to God's love towards him can now safely be expressed in the concern which he shows for others. That concern has been delivered from the peril of weariness, frustration, disappointment, despair, and ineffectiveness, each of which tragically prevents or damages external manifestations of a man's inner spirit. Each of them can frighten him into thinking that perhaps after all "it will not work out," or "it does not matter," or "there's something silly about giving oneself to people and causes when there is no genuine assurance of results."

I have insisted on a Christian's concern for the "big issues" of our day. But we must not forget what was said earlier, that it is easy to be so interested in these, precisely because of their enormous contemporary importance, and forget or do less than justice to our more immediate personal relationships. The old saying has it that "charity begins at home"; like so many trite aphorisms, it is true. I have known, as my readers must also have known, zealous workers for good in the affairs of society at large who were quite simply horrible people in their relationship with those closest to them. It seemed that they had "no time" for such small matters when they were occupying themselves with the big issues of the day. Such an attitude is absurd, un-Christian, and a visible sign that these people (if they were Christians by profession) were not growing in, but moving away from, life in Christ. Perhaps this is one of the practical reasons for the essential rightness of John's beginning with attention to the community immediately known to those who were to read his letter.

In one of his poems Rudyard Kipling said that "God gave each man all earth to love," but that "since our hearts are small" he also "gave to every man a little place / To love the best of all." We are given "all earth to love"; God loves like that and it is his intention that we should too. But our hearts are indeed "small"—not only because they are sinful and so often in the wrong, but also because they are finite, limited, conditioned by circumstance. We have our existence in *this* place, under *these* conditions, with *these* people. We must begin where we are and with those whom we know best, before we can embark on grand tours and engage ourselves in great enterprises. You can usually tell what a man really is, by observing how he relates himself to and behaves with those who are close at hand. If this is the case in ordinary human experience, it is all the more true of the life in Christ. The disciple who is genuinely growing in grace, deepening his relationship with his Lord, and letting Christ "dwell in his heart by faith," will show this in his contacts with the people near him, his family, his friends, those whom he loves, his close neighbors and associates in business or school or shop or plant. Then as opportunity is given or as demand requires, he will seek for and find wider spheres of expression for his deep concern for others in more remote places and for the great causes which properly may engage his interest and need his support.

For every one of us, life is a road we must walk here in this world. For the Christian, life in Christ is the *way* which God has made available for us in this walking in the world. The Christian is *on* that way. He too is a man; he too must tread the road which is human life. But for him there is something else too. The way for him is life in Christ. Nor does he need to climb up into the heavens to find that way, since (as Augustine so beautifully said) "the way has come to us." Jesus called himself, according to John's Gospel, "The Way, which is both truth and life" (I translate the familiar words in a slightly different manner from the accustomed one, since in the original Greek the double use of *kai,* or "and," signifies "both . . . and"). He is the way in which the Christian walks; it is the way of life and it is the way of truth, the true way for men. Augustine, who said that "the way has come to us," went on to say, "Let us then walk in it."

Life in Christ is walking in the way which is Christ. It is the way of love, for those close at hand and for those afar off, for little things and for big causes. It is shown for what it is, by what it leads us to do, in personal relations and in the wider concerns of our day.

9

The Goal of Life in Christ

IN THIS LAST CHAPTER OUR SUBJECT IS THE GOAL OR END of life in Christ.

The word "end" has two meanings in common usage. Perhaps most often we say it when we are thinking of *finis:* "This is the end; there isn't any more." But sometimes we say it when we are thinking of the goal in view, the purpose which is ours, the aim towards which we strive. In the former sense, it is a full stop; in the latter, it is an answer to the question, "What am I doing and why am I doing it?"

These two meanings are to be distinguished one from the other, lest we find ourselves creating much confusion when we speak. Yet there are occasions when both meanings may be included in our thought. The *final goal* is what we may be talking about. It is final because, so far as the road we are now taking is concerned, we have arrived at our destination; it is goal because it is the achievement for which we have been striving and the key to the work we have done.

I have entitled this chapter "The Goal of Life in Christ" because our chief concern in it will be the purpose which is ours and the aim towards which we are striving. But the other sense of the word "end" will not be forgotten, since we need always to take seriously our hoped-for point of arrival. Both are important for us. If we have no goal in view, no "end" in that sense, we shall live aimless lives; but if there is no terminus at which we hope to arrive we shall feel that we are wandering around like lost children, "strangers and afraid, in a world we never made."

Once more we shall find it helpful to begin by recalling something that Paul says in his letters. In Romans (8:28), the Apostle writes as follows, "We know that God in everything works towards a good end for those who love him and who are called according to his purpose." That is a better translation of Paul's Greek than the more familiar one in the Authorized Version: "All things work together for good to them that love God . . . ." In the Greek sentence, as commentators point out, *God* is the subject of the verb "work" or "work together." The mistaken translation, or at least the misleading one, in the Authorized Version is responsible for a considerable amount of misunderstanding of the Apostle's saying, and it has caused worry and disappointment to those who took it as it stood in the translation. It has also forced many theologians and preachers to resort to extraordinary feats of religious acrobatics to explain it or explain it away. In one sense, of course, all things *do* work for good for those who love God. That is to say, whatever happens can be turned into an occasion for good by those who see God's loving hand in all the happenings of their lives. But what the Apostle was telling his Roman correspondents was that *God* is the agent who in every aspect of our lives and in all the conditions under which we live is energizing in such a way that good will come of it. And we can apply here our two meanings of "end"; for when Paul speaks of the "good end" he intends to say that this good will be both the goal towards which we strive and the purpose in our striving and *also* the terminus to which God is bringing us as we walk in the Christian way.

When Paul says that God "works" towards "a good

end in every respect for those who love him," he is not to be understood as picturing God after the model suggested by a power-mad dictator or even by a benevolent tyrant. In an earlier chapter this false picture of God has been discussed and dismissed as contradictory to the Christian conviction that God has disclosed himself in Christ as he really is: a loving Father, although not an *easygoing* one. The latter idea would go against the entire Jewish view of fatherhood, in which Jesus was brought up and to which he appealed. A Jewish father would be stern, but his sternness was the demanding concern of one who loved his children. He expected the best from them and would not be satisfied with less than that, although because he *was* their father he accepted and loved them in any case. The revelation of God's fatherhood in the total impact of Jesus upon men went beyond this, however. In the light of that impact, the old Hebrew word *chesed* (God's loving-mercy, which the Jewish prophets had stressed) took on a new intensity. God was tender, like the father in the Parable of the Prodigal Son; he went out to seek and save his lost children, like the shepherd of whom Jesus told. Hence in his working in the world, he would not act in an arbitrary fashion, even if that might appear to be for the good of his children.

When we read Romans 8:28 in its context, we see that the Apostle is anxious to provide reassurance for Christians who may be troubled about their progress towards "the mark of their high calling," the goal which is also the terminus of their pilgrimage as they live in Christ and walk in his way. So he tells them that since God always works for a good end, and in every respect, for those who love him, they can be assured that he will not "let them down." He has called them, Paul says; he has accepted them, knowing who and what they are; even now he is so relating them to himself that they are being sanctified or empowered by his Spirit. Therefore they can trust that he will "glorify them"—bring them to their intended and destined terminus and thus establish their purposed goal. This is high encouragement; and the contemporary disciple has every right to take it to himself. For what Paul is saying may be paraphrased in this way: "My dear Christian friends in Rome, you already know something of the love of God because you already know Christ. You have responded a little to that love by a returning love to God as Christ reveals him. So do not be down-hearted because of your failures, serious as they seem to you, serious as they may be in themselves. Do not be downcast or dejected. God is able to fulfil his purpose for you and in you. Even now he is doing this, working in every way to bring you to himself, which is your ultimate goal. Carry on bravely and joyfully, then, even when you are in anguish and sorrow. Your job is to continue as a 'man in Christ.' Do not think of resting back on your oars or taking the easy way, for God expects you to do everything in your power, by your decisions and your actions, towards that goal. But in the last resort, you can be confident that God will see this thing through and will bring you to the place where all along he has purposed for you to be. He will give you the victory."

Here we have both terminus and goal. This is the goal of life in Christ; this is the point of our arrival. .

In recent years, some of us have been very much helped in our thinking about the Christian faith by a philosophical view associated with the name of the Anglo-American philosopher Alfred North Whitehead, from whom I have already quoted several times in this book. I believe that some of Whitehead's ideas can be of assistance to us as we think about the subject under discussion in this chapter. Furthermore, those ideas are so simple, and in a way so obvious, that the plain man can grasp them as readily as can the learned scholar.

Whitehead believed that everything in the world, from the tiniest bit of energy up to man himself, has an aim—a purpose it is meant to realize. But where does the aim come from? Whitehead said that the aim is "supplied by God." From the inexhaustible realm of possibilities, each has received by God's act its specific aim—we might almost say, its vocation. We are not able to see this clearly at the lower levels of the creation; but in human experience it becomes plain and there it is indeed a vocation given to each man. And what is that aim? It is the making actual and real of our manhood. We are to become what God calls us to become: true men, in every aspect of our being. The past which we inherit provides us material for this. The present in which we live challenges us and nourishes us—challenges us to make right choices and nourishes us by our relationship with others and with the world. The future is before us and offers us the goal, the fulfilment of the purpose of our existence.

Whitehead says that the initial aim supplied by God is to become, through our own decision and action, what he styles our own "subjective aim." In other words, we are to accept our calling and then choose and act in terms of it. We are responsible for the decisions we make as we receive from the past and are influenced by the many pressures of the present. But all the while, God is luring us, inviting us, soliciting us, trying to persuade us to move in the direction he intends us to follow.

Now let us apply this picture to our life as men in Christ. God has called us through Christ; he has given us our aim or goal of growing up in that life; he continually invites us and helps us on our way. We are not striving alone; the Holy Spirit is always there to strengthen and refresh us. We can boldly accept our calling and be "fellow-workers" with God in his never-ending activity in the world—or in Whitehead's word which we have used once or twice before, we can see that we are indeed "co-creators" with God. Having seen and known this, we must then act upon it. And we have the assurance that if we earnestly endeavor "to work out our own salvation in fear and trembling," as Paul once put it, "God works in

us to will and to do of his good pleasure." For the
Christian disciple, this is what life is meant to be; it is
what life is about. The English poet W. H. Auden has told
us, in his lovely "For the Time Being" (*The Christmas
Oratorio*), that *time,* in which we exist, is the "when" in
which this maturing in the reconciled life occurs; and that
space is the "where" in which it takes place. What light
that throws upon Christian discipleship in any time and
in any place!

But the Apostle is even bolder, for in the following
verses of that eighth chapter of the letter to the Christians in Rome he dares to say that the whole world, the
cosmos itself, is also called to a goal, is headed towards a
terminus. Let us hear his words: "The creation itself
waits with eager longing for the revealing of the sons of
God; for the creation has been subjected to futility, not
of its own will but by the will of him who subjected it in
hope; because the creation itself will be set free from its
bondage to decay and obtain the glorious liberty of the
children of God. We know that the whole creation has
been groaning in travail together until now; and not only
the creation, but we ourselves, who have the first-fruits of
the Spirit, groan inwardly as we wait for the adoption as
sons . . . ."

What are we to make of this? If we center attention on
the ·big point he is making, rather than on specific details,
we can see that the Apostle is affirming that the cosmos
or world is a creative movement *from* meaninglessness
("futility"), with its possible collapse into "bondage to
decay," *towards* fulfilment in accordance with God's
purpose. At the moment, he admits, the world may seem
futile and aimless; but that is *only* an appearance. God
has created it, is creating it day by day, in expectation of
its being brought to a terminus and made to achieve a
goal. And the human race, Paul says, is part of that
tremendous process, for in men have appeared its "first-
fruits," the foreshadowing or the initial installment of

what is to be the overall conclusion of the ongoing creative movement. And what is that conclusion? Paul says it is "the glorious liberty of the children of God." Of course that means in the first place men who are genuinely free because they are glad servants of God's love; but it can be extended, and the Apostle evidently means it to be so, to mean that the creation itself will be included in that "glorious liberty." For both men and the creation, such liberty is not the doing of what one wishes, as and when one wishes; that would be the most terrible bondage, for it would make men and creation subject to the impulses of the moment. The liberty meant here is exactly what Augustine, centuries ago, said it was: "the greater liberty" which is the unfailing free choice by each agent of the highest and best good for himself and for the world as a whole.

This is a magnificent vision. It is not to be dismissed, as some have been ready to do, as a flight of fancy or a bit of inspired poetry. Poetry it is; but it is poetry which like all great poetry speaks truth higher and truer than ordinary prose. And one of the contributions the vision makes to the man who is living in Christ is to be found in its putting his own life, apparently so small and insignificant, in the context of a cosmic drama, in which he is an actor whose role is important to God as he works out the sequence of events.

We have now indicated what the goal or purpose of life in Christ means. We have pointed to the place of arrival or terminus. We now ask, What *is* the place of arrival; and where is it?

Obviously that reference to "place" is not quite the way to phrase the question, for spiritual things are not in a place which can readily be located. Yet it *is* possible to speak of the "where" of the goal's "end." And the answer to the question is then simple. The point towards which human life and the cosmos are moving is God himself. Above all, the terminus of life in Christ is God.

To get a glimpse of the significance of the answer, however, we need to consider a little more God's way in his world and his relationship with the world.

We have said, following the thought of Whitehead, that God supplies or provides the "initial aim" or vocation of every creature. Now we must stress something that is equally important: God is the ultimate recipient of everything that happens in his world and to his creatures. To put this in the simplest way, we can say that God is affected (dare we not say influenced?) by the world of which he is the creator and sustainer. It is odd that many of the greatest Christian theologians have not been able to affirm this, for after all the Scriptures tell us over and over again how God rejoices or suffers from what goes on in his creation. The Bible is bold enough to picture God as One who cares enough to be deeply affected by what happens in the world he loves and to men whom he loves so dearly. Maybe the trouble with the theologians of whom I have just spoken is that they have sometimes allowed that glorious biblical picture of God to be too much contaminated by alien ideas derived (for the most part) from Greek philosophy with its notion that only the absolutely unaffected, uninfluenced, and unconcerned *could* be called "perfect." The Bible's idea is different from that: in Scripture God's perfection is his faithful character, his unfailing love, his unchanging purpose, not some abstract idea of "absolute immutability."

But however this may be, the way the Bible pictures God is as One who enjoys and delights in the good wrought in his creation, and who is in anguish when evil is done or wrong committed. Of course he is *always* God, unsurpassed and unsurpassable by anything else; of course he is always worshipful and supreme. And of course in him the joy of certain triumph is victorious over the anguish he feels at the world's evil and wrong. Yet he is also always affected by his world. In his inner experience, if we may be bold enough to use that almost blasphemous phrase, God rejoices in good, suffers from wrong, and is saddened when he must reject what is wrong, though he can make the occasion of wrong into an occasion for new good. And he rejoices all the more when there is a conscious, glad, and free response by men to his own outgoing love.

And now we can get a glimpse of the "where" which is the terminus and the goal of the life in Christ.

That life is a good thing now, as everyone who shares in it will agree. It is good enough to grow into greater fulness. And it is good enough to be received by God and to become part of his great joy, giving him delight and providing something that he can use for still further good in the world.

To have been permitted in this fashion to make a contribution to God's joy is a privilege beyond all comparison. The assurance given those who live in Christ is that nothing so good can ever be lost. It finds its terminus and its goal in God, but that is not the *end* of it; it does not have a "full stop." And why? Because God himself *never* has a stop. He is "from everlasting unto everlasting," not above all time and succession as if these were matters of indifference to him, but inclusive of time and succession in what some contemporary theologians have suggested might be styled "God's eminent temporality," from which all the imperfections and defects of time as we know it are removed. If our life in Christ is taken up into God, in this sense, it will continue in him for so long as God continues—and that is forever.

There is a frequent use in the Old Testament of phrases like God's "remembering," and their synonyms. Nehemiah prays that God will "remember" him, for example. This conception is singularly interesting and we should bear it in mind. Even for us, to remember something or someone is to give to the thing or person remembered a certain renewal of life. We often speak of how, when we remember, this or that "comes alive to us." In God, who so identifies himself with his creation that he knows everything in it as immediately present to him, "memory" must be immeasurably richer, fuller, and deeper than anything in our tiny finite experience. For God to remember is not only to make "come alive" but to keep alive forever. Whatever is thus received and accepted by God is safe forever; it can never come to an end, never have a stop.

This brings us to the final consideration in this chapter and in this book as a whole. Despite the efforts of many philosophers, there is no absolute proof of what we usually call "immortality." Most of the presuppositions on which, say, Socrates based his demonstration of such immortality are no longer entertained today. The arguments from "spiritualism," or supposed contacts with the spirits of the departed, are hardly convincing to many of us. The basic datum or ground for any such belief must be found elsewhere. And the Christian, who would speak (or should speak, if he remembers biblical usage) about resurrection rather than immortality, has an additional datum. This is the raising of Jesus Christ "from among the dead," as the credal phrase means literally. But even so, the Scriptures speak of "the *hope* of the resurrection," so far as you and I are concerned. This is no matter of demonstration or logical certainty; it is the confident and eager expectation of those whose life in Christ is now so real, so full, so enriching, that it is inconceivable that it can be destroyed. It is the Christian disciple's trust that he will share in what the creeds call "the communion of saints," those who are so knit together and so participant in God that they live forever, in some fashion which has not been revealed to us in our present limited human state, in God himself.

But having said that, it is equally important to go on to say that this Christian hope cannot be held in a "dog-in-the-manger" attitude. By this I mean the attitude of the man who says to God, "Unless you plainly prove to me that *I* shall live forever, I will not do your will, work for your cause, or serve my brethren." That attitude is so utterly un-Christian that it is hard to see how anybody could take it; yet some have done so. A person who does adopt such an attitude has not even begun to live the life in Christ; "he is still in his sin." For sin *is* self-willed insistence on one's own ways and one's own desires, carried to the point of defiance of God. Such a person therefore needs to be converted, so that he can see that everything in the world is meant to be to *God's* "greater glory," as the old phrase has it.

And so, last of all, we may ask, What *is* God's glory? Certainly if we trust the disclosure of himself given in Jesus Christ, we can say at once that it is not proud boasting, vaunting of himself, demanding from his creatures a cringing subservience. On the contrary it is solely and simply his boundless love, in all its mystery and wonder, as it declares itself in loving actions—this is so "glorious" that it evokes the response of worship and adoration and praise. To be caught up into God is to share his glory, in the most wonderful sense of the word. We have not been told precisely how this will be brought about for the man who lives in Christ. We should not be able to understand it if we were told, since we are limited in knowledge, imperfect in vision, and unable to grasp the deep mysteries of God as he is in himself. But we can say this.

We can say that to share in God's glory will be that same life in Christ which in all our unworthiness we have already been permitted to experience, but it will be that same life brought to its utter perfection. To share in God's glory will be more and more of what even now the Christian knows; it will not be something entirely different from what he now knows. There will be a continuity, as there will also be a difference. The difference will be that *then* awareness of God's love in Christ will be at its highest power—if you will, a difference in degree so great

that it will have become a difference in kind. It will be
life in Christ, life in grace, life in the Spirit, shared with
our brethren who are also in Christ and with the whole
redeemed and reconciled creation. To be assured of *that*
ought to be enough; and when one is assured of it, the
grateful response can only be, "Thanks be to God for his
unspeakable gift!"